BREAKTHROUGH

"One of the Church's most effective evangelists and entertainers (and those are by no means mutually exclusive categories), Fr. Rob Galea shares his remarkable life with us in his first book. Along the way, we learn lessons about faith and forgiveness, suffering and hope, laughter and tears. Open these pages to find out why he's one of the most well-known and beloved priests on the world stage today."

Rev. James Martin, S.J.

"Fr. Rob Galea invites us into his ongoing journey of encountering Christ and shows us how this encounter can be life-changing and fruitful if we open ourselves to the love of Jesus. A timely reminder of the hope we are offered in our deepest and darkest times!"

Curtis A. Martin
Founder and CEO of FOCUS

"Contemporary culture compels approaches to evangelization that are new in ardor, method, and expression. Fr. Rob Galea's efforts to reach young people with the saving power of the Gospel exemplify all three, and in his new book, he reveals precisely where his zeal for the mission originates—in a personal relationship with Jesus Christ, who is living, present, and accessible to all people in his Church."

Most Rev. Robert Barron
Auxiliary Bishop of Los Angeles

"Fr. Rob's vulnerability and authenticity are refreshing, his story is encouraging, and his love for the Lord is an inspiration to anyone who seeks Jesus and desires to give their life to him."

Katie Prejean McGrady
Author of *Follow*

BREAKTHROUGH
FR. ROB GALEA

A JOURNEY FROM DESPERATION TO HOPE

AVE MARIA PRESS AVE Notre Dame, Indiana

All scripture quotations, unless otherwise indicated, are taken from the Holy Bible, New International Version®, NIV®. Copyright ©1973, 1978, 1984, 2011 by Biblica, Inc.™ Used by permission of Zondervan. All rights reserved worldwide. www.zondervan.com The "NIV" and "New International Version" are trademarks registered in the United States Patent and Trademark Office by Biblica, Inc.™

Original edition published in Australia by
Garratt Publishing
32 Glenvale Crescent
Mulgrave, VIC 3170

www.garrattpublishing.com.au

Foreword © 2017 by Liam Lawton

Founded in 1865, Ave Maria Press is a ministry of the United States Province of Holy Cross.

www.avemariapress.com

Paperback: ISBN-13 978-1-59471-837-3

E-book: ISBN-13 978-1-59471-838-0

Cover image © Edward Dingli.

Cover design by Samantha Watson.

Text design by Andy Wagoner.

Printed and bound in the United States of America.

This book is dedicated to all people young and old that they may be encouraged to seek out and live in the truth of God's unconditional love.

CONTENTS

Foreword

As the morning sun is rising somewhere in the world, it is also setting on another part of this beautiful planet. One half sleeps while the other half begins their daily chores of living, working, and dreaming.

No matter where you go in this world, the human heart is the same. The hopes and dreams of all humans are to belong, to be loved, and to succeed. We are all the same, though we may not know it. What we also do not know is that we are all part of the beautiful dream of God—each and every one. Why, every hair on our head has been counted (see Matthew 10:30), as God the Father, who loves each person equally, calls us into the fullest life possible.

Each life is unique. Each life can never be replaced. Each life is precious. We all have our own stories to tell, no matter how diverse, different or shocking. Each of us is loved and accepted by God as if we were the only ones that existed in the world. To appreciate such diversity and difference it is not only good but important that we hear and listen to each other's stories. There is something wholesome and healing about learning from the joys and sorrows of other lives and how God reaches out to them and to us *through* them.

Fr. Rob Galea is no exception. His story, though unique, is also the story of God's abounding love for us as he heals and restores us and points us in the direction that will bring us the meaning of life and the peace of mind that we seek.

This is a story of strife and searching, it is a story of refining and redemption, but it is also a story of great love—the love of a mother for her son, the love of a family for an angst-filled teenager, the love of a community for one of their own, and above all, the love of a God for his child. It is about joy and sorrow. It is not without struggle and sadness, but it is also very much about the triumph of the human heart and the manifestation of God's holy spirit: real and active in our world today.

If God can call someone from the idyllic sun-kissed stones of Malta to serve in far-off Australia—and lead him through a world of fame and fortune, through the bright lights of TV and screen—to find meaning in the sufferings and struggles of the poor, the prisoner, the unloved, the lost ones; what could he not do with so many more of us who would offer their lives and hearts to him, who loves us so much?

As I read this book, I was moved. I wondered at the ability of the human heart to know so much suffering and yet so much love when we allow Jesus to help us and heal us. It challenged me, one who is also in ministry, to acknowledge my trust or lack of trust in Jesus' desire to lead and direct my life, broken and all as it is. I have no doubt that it will be the same for all who dare to turn the pages and read.

We live in a world that cries out for revenge and retribution without knowing that the real cry within our hearts is a cry to know, love, and serve God in each other. This search for love is sadly manifested through addictions of all kinds: through a desire for fame and popularity, through the belief that only the strongest and most able should survive. The vulnerable and weak, the poor and deprived have no place at the table of modernism. What is said in this book is the antidote to such belief. It shows us that our search is a search for God, though we do not know it. As St. Augustine said in *Confessions* about God, "our heart is restless until it rests in you."

In this book, Fr. Rob Galea shows us the remedy to the pain and paranoia that modern living brings. It is a book about making peace with one's self and one's neighbor but framed by the love of God and his abiding presence. "God never gives up" is a subtitle that I would give this book. Ultimately, it is a book about trust—trusting in God, step by step, little by little, day by day, until one day we can jump off the cliff and into his waiting arms.

This is a book that all young people should have an opportunity to read. In the story of Jesus, he invites his friends and those who wondered about him to "come and see" and eventually to "come and follow" him. It is a brave step to take in today's world. It won't promise fame and fortune. It won't promise happiness and security as the world knows it, but what it will promise is repayment a thousand times over in fulfilment and the satisfaction of knowing and trusting in the God of love, in his son Jesus, and the opportunity to bring that love to a waiting world.

Perhaps this is the *breakthrough* that *you* too have been waiting for.

Fr. Liam Lawton
Roman Catholic priest and singer

The Phone Call

B efore I was on *The X Factor Australia*, before I performed for a pope, before I signed a record deal, and before I picked up a guitar and sang in front of a crowd for the first time, I was an alienated, messed-up teenager.

Hi, my name is Rob. My mother calls me "Robert" and my parishioners call me "Fr. Rob." I find it surreal being called "Father," especially by people who are old enough to be my grandparents. My own late grandfather used to call me "Father" even though I asked him many times just to call me by my name. In my own mind, I am simply "Rob," but my proper title is "Fr. Rob" as I was ordained a Catholic priest on the fifth of November, 2010.

I never imagined myself serving God and the Church as a priest, and never did I think I would be carrying out my ministry so far away from home! I work in a place called Bendigo, a country town of 100,000 people in the state of Victoria, Australia, 15,570 kilometres from Malta, which is where I grew up.

Even though I fly all over the world now, performing in front of hundreds of thousands of people every year, in my heart and soul, there's a part of me that's still the introverted, terrified person I was as a teenager.

By the time I was sixteen, I'd created my own little circle of hell. I was trapped. Anyone who's been there knows how hard it is. I was literally hiding in my room from dangerous people who I thought were friends. I couldn't escape my problems and I didn't know where to turn for help. I was lost, alone, and on the verge of doing something drastic. I cried myself to sleep and woke up every morning soaked in self-hatred, thinking about ways to end my life. Locked alone in my room, rocking back and forth, I wished for some way to stop the pain that consumed me but could see no way out. It felt like I'd reached the end of myself. I wanted it all to end.

But to my surprise, I got out of my dark little room, and I did it with help from an unexpected source: God.

≈

Before I get too far ahead of myself, let me explain how I got into such a dark place.

I grew up in Malta. My parents—especially my mother—went to church. Religion is a big deal in Malta. It's one of the most Catholic places on earth; Roman Catholics make up the majority of the population, there's a Catholic government, and as many churches on street corners as coffee shops in Melbourne.

Like everyone in Malta, I went to a Catholic school. And like everyone, I didn't always get along with my peers. I was mocked, bullied, and I often went home in tears. My father tried his best to intervene with the school and the bullies, but the abuse didn't stop. I began to look for ways to skip school. I would fake an illness, or if I couldn't do that, I would make myself throw up at school so they would send me home. I even changed schools to get away from it all, but by then I was convinced that I couldn't do anything right.

In my mind, I was not worth the effort.

So I shut out the world. My teenage years didn't get much better. I was drinking and smoking, and what friends I did have couldn't understand the fascination for these new and enticing substances. I just wanted to be different.

Drinking led to smoking pot, which led to experimenting with harder stuff. When I was high, I felt a little more accepted, a little more loved. It was the same with shoplifting. It started out as a cry for attention which then became an uncontrollable addiction. Eventually, I couldn't walk into a shop or go to a friend's house without taking something.

I started hanging out with a group of older guys who had money, exuded confidence, and demanded respect. Some people might have called these new friends "thugs." They carried knives and knuckledusters. One friend, the son of a major drug dealer, brought a handgun to school once. These guys picked fights for no reason. I had close calls where I thought people were looking to kill me because of these guys.

And then there was the lying. The only place I felt truly accepted was in my inner make-believe world. In this imaginary cocoon, I had all the love and acceptance I could ever want. I spent so much time in this bubble that I would even talk to friends and family about girls I had dated and adventures I had, believing the events I made up were true. I told so many lies that it got hard to see the difference between a lie and the truth, and I hated myself for it.

The reality was that I hated my life, and I believed that the whole world felt the same way about me that I did.

Eventually, lying got me into the biggest trouble of my life. I told a lie about a drug dealer's son, the head of the gang that I was hanging out with. He had a girlfriend, but I told people I'd seen him with another girl. I was so delusional that I saw it in my head and believed it had happened. I was in a club with friends when someone came in and told me that the guy found out what I'd said and was now looking for me. I was terrified. I ran home and woke up my parents, begging them to hide me because these guys were going to hurt me. The same group had attacked a friend of mine;

his head had been smashed on a hotel door so hard that he ended up in intensive care.

That paralysed me. It sent me to a place where I was terrified and depressed. A mutual friend negotiated a truce so that the gang would leave me alone but only if I stayed away. That was fine with me. I didn't want to go out even if I could.

And that's how I became that guy, trapped in my room. I stopped seeing people. I stopped doing anything. It worried my mother so much that she took me to see various priests around town, desperately seeking their advice and care, hoping it would help, but it didn't.

There was no hope left for me.

Week after week, I stayed in my room. Darkness was my only friend.

Then the phone rang and everything changed.

≈

Miracles don't always look like miracles. The miracle that saved me from myself all those years ago started with a phone call. There was no way I could have known it at the time, but that call has led me to where I am today: wearing a priest's black shirt and white collar, devoting my life to God, and trying to connect with people. I have given my life to reach teenagers like the one I once was.

To this day, I'm still an introvert. I'd much rather stay in my room than preach. Every time I have to I speak, I get tense, and public speaking is my full-time job! It doesn't even matter how often I do it—I still get terrified right before Sunday Mass. Yet every week, I do it scared. I push my fear aside because I have work to do.

These days, a lot of people know me from my concerts and talks, seeing my performance on *The X Factor*, or by following me on YouTube, Instagram, or Twitter. It's amazing, really, all of this attention, but I have no interest in fame or being known for myself. I do it to make God known and loved in a personal way by those who want to know about him. I try to show people what it means to love God, and if it means I have to go out onto a stage to sing or talk, despite being an introvert, I do it. Don't get me wrong, I love what I do, and I don't want to sound like a martyr. There are a lot of crosses to bear, but I do it gladly because I know how much good it does. Jesus is my "first love" (see Revelation 2:4), and I will sing his praise to anyone who will listen.

During the week, I work like any other assistant parish priest: saying Mass, celebrating weddings and conducting funerals, and visiting people at the parish where I live or at other parishes in the diocese of Sandhurst, which is so big it takes more than four hours to drive from one end to the other. I also lead Stronger Youth, the local diocese's youth ministry. This puts me in front of thousands of high school and college students around the state of Victoria every year. On weekends, I become Fr. Rob, "the singing priest": performing concerts, appearing at speaking engagements around Australia and the world, and using YouTube, Instagram, and Snapchat to share lessons on what it means to know, love, and serve Jesus.

Even though I've been doing this for years, I still haven't come to terms with the fact that I swoop in, speak to hundreds or even thousands of people, and then move on to the next performance in what feels like a blink of the eye. It's often a hit-and-run ministry, and it can be frustrating not having enough time to connect with the people I encounter on a deeper level.

I'd like to say I have it all together, but I don't. I'm still at the beginning of my journey. My greatest hope is that you will walk toward God with me, so you can catch a glimpse of what I believe it means to be a follower and a disciple of Jesus.

That's why I've created this book for you. My hope is that it will be a resource for those who've attended my talks or concerts and for anyone else who wants to get on their feet and walk with God and the Catholic community. If you're anything like I was when I was young and looking for stability or direction or a way out of darkness, then I hope this book will plant the seed of discipleship with Jesus in your heart.

While working in Australia, I've encountered many families who have up to four generations of non-practicing Catholics: families from the great-grandparents on down who have never stepped inside a church except, as they say, to "hatch, match, and dispatch." (That is, to get baptized, get married, or carry out a funeral.) I've spoken with those who have told me of a fall-out with another parishioner or clergy, a loss of faith in God, or disengagement with the liturgy; sometimes the effort and distance needed to travel to get to a church on Sundays has played a role in that dis-engagement. In writing this book, I want to help them—and you—understand that a search for love away from God is a search that leads away from what our hearts and souls are looking for. I want nothing more than to see Jesus find a place in your heart once more.

The book includes milestones in my life that brought me closer to God. I'm hoping that the lessons I've learned can help others who've been through the same trials or that it might assist people who are helping someone they love through similar rough patches. Prayer and music are big parts of my life, so I've included both to use as prompts for reflection. At the end of each chapter, I want you to reflect on what we've discussed and how it might apply to your life. You might also like to keep your Bible on standby to look up and bookmark your favorite passages and those quoted in my story. I use the New International Version (NIV), but don't worry too much if yours isn't the same. The important thing is that you have a Bible and keep it nearby.

And I have something special for you. Just for reading this book, you get access to an exclusive section of my website where you can listen to some of my music and watch a few videos. In each chapter you'll find a QR code which will lead you to the extra content. All you need to do is use your QR Code Reader app on your smartphone and you'll be taken directly to the special content. You might even choose to listen to the songs as you read each chapter.

≋

Back to that fateful phone call in Malta. It was an invitation to come to a youth group meeting at a church in Balzan, not far from St. Andrews, where I lived. Actually, the invitation wasn't even for me; it was for my sister, Rachel. I wasn't particularly religious at that point, but I was insulted not to be included and said so.

One thing led to another and I ended up at the meeting. While I was there, I heard someone talk about having a personal relationship with God. How wonderful that sounded! To have a direct connection to someone, to God, who could understand me and what I was going through!

Afterward, I went home, and went back to being scared and isolated my room.

Only this time, something was different. I was ready for a change.

I put an empty chair across from me and talked to it as if someone were sitting there. Day after day I talked. Day after day nothing happened.

Then one day, someone talked back.

While I had a great childhood, my teenage years were difficult.

ONE

Surrender

I was born in the 1980s, in a time of great political unrest in Malta. There were tensions between the government and the opposing party, as well as the Church. I was too young to really understand what was happening, but I remember playing at home and my parents worrying that it was not safe to go out. Somehow, they shielded my siblings and me from this political unease. My early childhood, as I remember it, was idyllic.

And how could it not be? Malta was a beautiful place to grow up. It's an archipelago in the middle of the Mediterranean Sea, about eighty kilometers south of Italy. It's rich in history and architecture and food, having hosted the navies of many great world powers from the Phoenicians through to the British. It also has the best climate in the whole world! Winters are mild and summers are perfect for getting out on the azure waters of the Mediterranean.

My family had a nice house in St. Andrews, a town on the north central side of the main island. My brother, sister, and I were brought up in a Catholic home, and we also followed some local traditions. On my first birthday, I took part in a Maltese tradition called *quċċija*, where a young child is presented with a silver tray full of items, and whichever item is chosen by the child is said to represent the type of life they are likely to have. There are many different items on the tray like rosary beads, an egg, a hammer, a calculator, and others. A hammer, for instance, would signify that a child might grow up to work with his or her hands. A rosary would signify following a religious path, and a calculator either IT or accounting.

I picked the hard-boiled egg, which signifies living life to the full—something I've certainly done so far!

Life was just so comfortable. My father, by twenty-three years of age, had worked long and hard enough to build us a large family home. And it had to be big! We had to house five people, our pet dog and cat, and some dwarf rabbits, as well as chickens and an aviary full of budgerigars and canaries. Some of my happiest childhood memories are set in that home with our animals.

My favorite pet was a boxer by the name of Rixu (pronounced *ree-shu*). Rixu was the friendliest dog, and whenever I was around him I felt completely safe. I used to love hanging out with him; we would just cuddle and chill out together. He was such a comfort to us, but one day he went missing. This broke our hearts. Anyone who's ever lost a pet can identify with our anxiety. We thought we were the luckiest family when we found him about six months later, but he had become aggressive and contracted an illness while on the streets. To my utter despair, we had to put him down. I was completely devastated, but he wasn't the only pet to put us through that trauma. We also had a cat that caused us heartbreak. Her name was Peisha. She suddenly went missing the week my brother was born, which was when I was around eight years old. My parents said she ran away, but it wasn't until years later that I found out that they got rid of her in order to protect my baby brother from any harm they thought she might cause.

Everything was an adventure back then. Every afternoon, my mother would take us children outside to wait for Dad to come home from work. We would all climb up on a big rock in the middle of a field just outside our property, and while we waited, we would watch the cows being walked back to the dairy farm after a day spent grazing in the field. Climbing and sitting on those rocks with Mum, Rachel, and Joseph was a beautiful and safe adventure.

My sister was born seventeen months after me. We used to argue a lot, but we were also the closest of friends. I remember we used to walk home from the bus stop after school. It was a long walk up a steep hill, and very tiring, but I would walk ahead of my sister, ring random doorbells and then run on ahead. The homeowners would open the door just as she went past, and what with me being well up the street, she would cop a torrent of abuse for being cheeky. She used to cry the rest of the way home but she always forgave me! It was so nice having a sister, and she was always plenty of fun.

We tried to have fun all the time. My sister and I used to wake up early and sneak into our parents' bed on a weekend. I'm sure Mum and Dad did not appreciate being woken up so early, but we used to have the most beautiful mornings. My sister and I, after our initial ambush, would often end up being wrestled and tickled by Dad, with Mum looking on in delight. My younger brother, Joseph, wasn't born when we first started doing this, but in time he joined us on our early morning weekend sneak-attacks.

We spent so many of our days outside or with family and friends. I remember sitting with my father's parents on a balcony at their summer house, overlooking a busy road, with the ocean in the distance. I would sit on my grand-mother's lap and together we would count the cars as they passed by the house. I would count the red cars and she would count the blue cars. My sister joined in, too, when she was old enough, counting the white cars, and then we would have a competition to see who could reach one hundred first. I remember this with great fondness. I was probably about six years old at the time.

When I was at home, I used to spend a lot of time playing on the streets and riding my bicycle. With my sister and our friends, we would go and explore the fields and the valleys close by. There was an abandoned building not far from our house and we used to go there regularly. It was full of graffiti and falling to pieces and would probably have been sealed off if it were still there today, but we used to climb the walls and hang out on the roof. That place had great views, and the air always felt so fresh on top of that building, almost like we were on top of the world.

We weren't exactly a rich family, but we were comfortable and we had each other. That's all any family can ask for, really. My dad owned a company that sold home furnishings. My mother is Maltese, but she grew up in England and Switzerland and moved back to Malta as a teenager, so we spoke English at home. Most Maltese people speak Maltese as their first language and English as a second language, and many, due to our close proximity to Italy, speak Italian too. We were like everyone else and spoke a bit of everything.

We were always so busy! We saw our grandparents often. Almost every Sunday they came over for Mum's baked pasta, a roast, or a barbeque. In summer, we would spend our days on the beach or sailing around the beautiful Maltese islands where we would attend Mass by the water on the island of Comino. At night, we would watch the incredible displays of fireworks in the villages on land from our boat on the ocean. We would never come home empty-handed from these excursions. We were often given lollies, soft toys, or Legos, and who doesn't love Legos at that age?

For some of our summer vacations, we went sailing on the family yacht to Italy, and all through the Mediterranean Sea, too. From every part of Malta you can see the ocean, so it was natural for us to spend plenty of time on the water. In fact, it wasn't until I was thirteen that I found out that not everyone could swim. It was unheard of in Malta, almost unbelievable, as water is a huge part of our cultural heritage.

After school in the summer months, kids would be sent straight to the beach to cool off. I remember on the last day of school every year, the day summer holidays began, I would run home with my brother and sister and jump in our pool with our school uniforms still on! It became a family tradition, and it was the perfect way to break the shackles of routine and really put us in the mood for holidays.

I really was brought up on the water; right in the belly of the big blue, perfect ocean that is the Mediterranean. I feel like the ocean is so ingrained in my being that when I came home for a visit after two years in my landlocked diocese in Australia, I was in utter disbelief at how beautiful it was. It was like a dream. In fact, the first thing I did was ask that my father take me out right away! It became clear that I had taken the ocean for granted in my youth. I have grown to appreciate it more now—I just love the water. I swim, snorkel, play water polo, and fish every chance I get.

We always had some kind of boat as I grew up. Our first boat was a small fiberglass number which had a tiny little five horsepower engine. I used to love hanging out with my father on that boat. We would go fishing in the bay of Xemxija (pronounced *shem-she-yah*). Eventually we upgraded to a speedboat. This allowed us to travel from our little bay to other beaches around the main island, and even across to the different Maltese islands with the whole family. Occasionally, we would wake up at 4 a.m. and go fishing in the boat. This was generally with my father and his factory workers and was an absolute treat. This instilled in me a great love for deep-water fishing, something I still love to this day. However, I still hate waking up at 4 a.m.!

We didn't always take out the boat. Sometimes we angled for mullets and other small fish off the beach near my grandparent's summer house. We would catch as many as we could, but we mostly threw them back in the water afterwards, leaving just enough to cook once we got home.

But fishing wasn't without its share of dangers. I remember on one occasion getting my finger caught in a fishhook. I think I was about twelve years old at the time. I didn't even realize I'd snagged my finger at first, I just felt a pull as I normally did. I actually thought I'd caught a fish, so I jerked the rod. Well, that was a mistake! The hook went deep into my finger, which led to a trip to the emergency department at breakneck speed. I ended up having the hook surgically removed. It was not an experience I'd care to repeat.

My parents sold the speedboat at about the same time as the fishhook incident, but not for that reason. They decided to buy a yacht which they named *Annie G*, after my mother. It was a three-bedroom yacht and from that point on we used it to sail across the Maltese islands every weekend throughout summer. We also spent at least one month at sea whenever my father had holidays. He later upgraded to a bigger and better boat that even had air-conditioning. That was fantastic. I used to spend hours fishing and zooming around different bays on the little tender of the yacht with my brother and sister. We had lots of fun on those long summer days.

I used to think that I would spend my life on the water. In it, under it or on it—it didn't matter. I just loved being outside, and I loved the sea. I think we've all probably got some sort of connection like that with nature. Because we had a boat, we would rarely travel overseas, except to go sailing to Sicily, which we did quite often. One winter, my parents decided to take the entire family on a holiday to London, England. It was a beautiful trip; the very first time I saw snow. I'd never seen anything like it; Malta just doesn't get that cold. I also think I put on about three kilograms that holiday eating nothing but cupcakes and brownies for breakfast.

Closer to home, Carnival was a big deal in Malta, and yet another thing I love about my beautiful island home. The streets would be filled with floats, color would be everywhere, and we would all dress up and head to Valletta, the capital city. Thousands of people would gather as we celebrated the joy of Carnival. The same would happen at Easter as big processions filled the street. Religion is important in Malta; Easter's a time of prayer and togetherness for the Maltese people. It's such a unifying time. Christmas is also widely and loudly celebrated, with holiday music playing on every street and in shops and churches. The main streets get covered in decorations and the Nativity is set up in every church. Malta is so joyous at these times.

I used to love spending time with my cousins during these big celebrations. We had a large extended family who would congregate at the major holidays. At Christmas time, we used to dress up and put on a play for our parents and grandparents. We were and still are a close family. Even today, all of my cousins are online, and we regularly communicate in group chat. Living so far away from them isn't easy, but with a good smartphone and handy messaging apps, the distance is nothing.

Life was so good. It was simple, and I was happy. I didn't really understand how much my parents had sacrificed to give us a happy and joyful childhood. My father was under a lot of pressure running a business, and like most businesses, it sometimes made profits and at other times made losses. When he was on the boat, or when we were away on holiday, it was like he was a different person. We all were.

With Mum and Dad there to protect us, I couldn't have asked for a better life.

≋

But things change.

As I started to grow up, life began to get a little more complicated. Things got dark.

As I alluded to earlier, I started getting bullied at school, and for the first time, my parents could not protect me. It got worse when my grandfather, and then my grandmother passed away within a short period. That was the first time I ever saw my father cry. I did not know how to deal with my grandmother's death in particular, and the grieving of my whole family, who I had always thought of as unshakable.

I was so angry and confused, and I didn't understand why things were changing. I didn't understand why things had to be so different and why people had to die. I wanted answers, and I needed the stability and bliss of my earlier life. I argued constantly with my parents, and in what I thought was retaliation, they put more and more restrictions on me. I would throw tantrums, break things, and fight with my sister and brother. Holidays were less fun, and I no longer felt special.

I told myself that I could not wait to move out of that house. I was fourteen years old.

I didn't realize back then that many people feel that way at fourteen. I thought that I was the victim, that nothing was my fault, and that everything was happening to me and me alone. I'm sure you can relate. Everything was cascading as I lurched from one problem to another. It seemed like things were getting worse and worse as I fought off bullies and personal grief.

I can see now that this problem had been building for a while, but at the time I was overwhelmed. I was reacting to every little situation instead of thinking it through. The world had been great when it was just my family and the beach and the water, but school changed everything. Going to school messed with my little utopia.

My first primary school was a private Catholic school for boys, St. Edward's College, one of the best in Malta. I did not enjoy my time there, even though it was a great institution. I was constantly mocked and bullied. The other kids made fun of my appearance and even though I tried to fight back, my attempts proved futile. I desperately wanted friends, but not a single classmate stood up for me. I changed schools to get away from it, but the damage was done. My self-esteem was wrecked. I was convinced that I was worthless.

I was tired of trying to please others and became terrified of failure and of disappointing my father in particular. I became introverted and angry. At the smallest sign of rejection, I'd have a tantrum and break things.

It didn't help that I wasn't the best athlete, so I couldn't redeem myself through sport. I was never any good at soccer. Whenever the ball came towards me, I would run away. It didn't help matters that all of my cousins seemed to be great athletes. In fact, one of them ended up swimming in the Olympics and another two played for Malta's national soccer team. When we were young, they all won trophies and medals for all kinds of sports. I, on the other hand, had no coordination skills whatsoever. It wasn't until I was in my early teens that I discovered that I could play water polo and that I was a decent swimmer, too. In fact, I travelled to Paris to represent my swimming club as a young teen. It was when I got back from Paris that I really started to rebel.

By the time I was fourteen years old, I only cared about heavy metal bands and clubbing. Our house was big enough that I could climb out of my bedroom window at night without anybody hearing. I'd walk to nightclubs in Paceville: a party zone not far away from my house that was dotted with bars, clubs, discos, casinos, bottle shops, and year-round revelry.

I started to wear band T-shirts, grew my hair long, and pierced an ear. My dad would not have approved had he known. I'd take my earring out when I came home from the club and then re-pierce it the next time I went out. Do you know how painful that was?

My fashion sense and rebellious behavior weren't the only areas where my dad and I disagreed. He was protective but strict. I can see now that he only wanted what was best for me, but at the time, the way he communicated his feelings seemed harsh and uncaring. To me, it felt like no matter how good I was, I could be better. I rebelled. My dad and I would argue about this frequently. One time we didn't talk for a whole month.

I really did want him to feel proud of me, but I had a constant fear of disappointing him, which led to me messing up. I'd study but never get the results he expected. He'd congratulate me but send me back to my room to study more.

I tried to fix a broken antique clock once. I dismantled it and tried to put it together again, but it took much longer than I expected, and was much more complex than I had ever imagined. I ended up in a serious panic when I heard my dad walk through the door. I was mortified when he stood over me as I sat with springs and screws all over the kitchen floor! He could not believe that I would intentionally destroy his valuable clock. Needless to say, I suffered the consequences.

I often tried to impress Dad with my knowledge, but I did that by contradicting him all the time. That was, in part, a facet of my search for my own identity and, consequently, my rebellion against authority, thinking that I knew everything. That used to frustrate him and cause both him and I to lose our tempers and start an argument. We were constantly fighting, and I didn't want to have to deal with it. Who does at that age? So I took my rebellion out of the house and onto the street.

When I think back now, I know that I was a good person with a good heart, but I was desperate for attention and the love that I thought I had stopped getting. It was obviously still there, but my mind was telling me otherwise. I was frustrated, but despite that, I don't think I ever lost my heart to help people, and to be good to people.

When I was fourteen years old and starting to lean into my rebellion with a vengeance, my parents went overseas for a trip. I stayed with my cousins and aunty and uncle, and the only way for me to get to school in the morning was with one of their neighbors. His name was Daniel. Daniel had muscular dystrophy and so he used to have a carer drive him to school every day. I would travel to school with them as it was easier for everyone involved, and I didn't have to inconvenience my aunt or uncle.

Daniel and I became close friends and eventually the best of friends. I spent a lot of time at his house just hanging out with him, going to the cinema and swimming. I would care for him at school and then after school at his house. We had sleepovers where I would turn him around at night because he couldn't turn himself. I would help him shower and go to the bathroom. I would dress him too, but I never saw myself as doing anything extraordinary. He was my friend, and that's what you did for a friend. I once won a prize at school for being the "most caring person" because of my love and care for Daniel. I even travelled to Sweden with him and his father on holiday one summer to assist with his care.

I knew I was a decent kid, and Daniel brought out the best in me.

But I wasn't with Daniel all the time. I was happy being Daniel's friend, but now that I was going to a school that was better for me, I also wanted to hang out with my other school friends at the nightclubs on the weekend.

Sometimes, I was my own worst enemy. I was a good person, but I was capable of bad things, too. I was right on the verge of toying with addiction.

In Paceville, I picked up smoking cigarettes. My preferred brand was Benson and Hedges Gold because they were the cheapest. Only a few of my friends smoked, but I saw that being one of those special few gave me extra attention, which I liked. It was easy to hide the smell when I got home because in the clubs everybody smoked. You could smell like smoke just by walking past the entrance of a club, or even standing a good ten meters away.

My mother once saw a pack of cigarettes in my bag. She didn't confront me about it at the time, but she saw that I saw. I'll never forget the pain and shock in her soft, blue-green eyes. Once she left my room, I leaned my head against my bedroom wall and covered my face in shame. The last thing I wanted to do was cause my mother pain, but I soon forgot about this incident. It wasn't enough to make me change my ways, and so I continued on with my prodigal lifestyle.

I drank a lot. Back then, the legal drinking age was sixteen, but even at fourteen, I could walk into any number of places and buy a drink whenever I wanted. I didn't have to worry about ID or anything.

The first drink I ever had at a nightclub was that very first night I jumped out of my bedroom window. I had just had an argument with my parents and got sent to my room. I waited for them to go to sleep, then I snuck out of the house and headed to the nightclub. Once I got there, I recognized an older friend who took me into the club with some of his mates. They were drinking beers. My mate cracked one open and handed it to me. I didn't even hesitate. I took the beer, but I did not like it *at all*. I somehow managed to finish it, but then my head began to spin.

I was losing my sense of self.

I'd no sooner finished the first one when my friend handed me another, and by the time I was halfway through *that* one I could barely move. I was hooked. It felt so good. I had all of these powerful emotions; I felt happy, and I felt extraordinarily confident. I did regret my drinking later that night, as you can no doubt imagine. I was not very well at all, but I was not sick enough to stay away from it.

I loved the feeling of acceptance from my peers in this new life. I could not get enough of it. One afternoon when I was walking through a supermarket with some friends, I decided to do something crazy to get their attention. With a racing heart and sweaty palms, I stole the first thing I saw and hustled outside. My prize: a bottle of vanilla extract from the baking aisle. I didn't care what I'd stolen. All I knew was I'd gotten away with it.

That led to more shoplifting: a pair of sunglasses, an electric toothbrush, clothes, money from a friend's house. Stealing made me feel powerful. It put me in control, but before too long, I'd lost all that control to a different addiction—the adrenaline rush. The thrill I got as I stole was so powerful, and the stuff I stole, well, I never used it. I just kept it in my room or threw it away.

I was starting to lose it. I craved even more popularity and attention. In the tenth grade, I started hanging out with a gang of older guys. They sported baggy pants, oversized T-shirts, Jordans shoes, and snapbacks (caps). They carried knives and knuckledusters. One boy, the son of a major drug dealer, brought a handgun to school, as I mentioned earlier. To this day, it's the only gun I've ever seen on Malta, outside of a hunting rifle.

Every moment I could spend away from home, I would. Alone or hanging out with friends, it didn't matter. I just wanted to be out of the house and away from the constant arguing with my parents. My friends and I would go to shopping centers and in the evenings sneak into nightclubs. I would drink and smoke and do drugs. When I was bored I would go into shops and steal stuff, useless things that I didn't even need. It gave me a thrill. It became my life.

On one occasion we were outside a Burger King, just hanging around, and a random guy ran by, going who knows where. Out of nowhere, someone in our group grabbed him, pushed him up against the wall and suddenly seven or eight people were beating him up. I often had to run away from trouble like that as, inevitably, the cops were called.

Yet despite all of this, I found this lifestyle fun. I was gaining popularity among my peers with every outrageous night out, even though in reality I was losing control of my thoughts, actions, and behavior. I didn't see it that way at the time. I felt that for the first time since my childhood, I had control of my life. I had power and respect as I transitioned from being bullied to becoming a bully. I felt invincible.

That was until my addictions and low self-esteem caught up with me.

It always does. I've come to learn over the years that everyone is held accountable for their actions in the end, and it often starts with a loss of control.

Before I knew it, my addictions were controlling me. I drank too often, stole too often, lied too often, and began fights too often. My aggression transcended the group I hung out with. I was a willing but terrible fighter. In the water I'm fine, I can move about like a graceful fish, but put me on dry land and I have no coordination. I would push people around at school and get my own back with a nasty concussion here and a broken finger there. Because of my aggression, constant lying, and troublemaking, my school and childhood friends no longer wanted to hang out with me, but still I persisted with this rebellious behavior.

Though I craved attention, drugs almost got me noticed in a way I didn't want. I was with a group who were smoking pot and the police showed up. My friends had me stuff the pot in my pocket because I was the most innocent-looking of the whole bunch. The police didn't search me so I got away with it. I got lucky.

And then there was the lying. I mentioned it already, how I had my own little world where life was perfect and where I was the hero, but when I told the biggest lie of my life, the one that led to my self-imposed exile, I hit rock bottom.

It had to happen eventually.

Having fabricated a story that cast one of my new, so-called "mates" in a bad light, I ended up running for my life. Who lies and says they saw their friend getting intimate with a girl who was not their girlfriend? I must have been crazy, because he found out about my lie and was out to hurt me. It was no idle threat on his behalf. If he had caught me, it would have been violent. I had nowhere to run but home.

I hid in my room, utterly terrified.

I was alone.

No friends. A tumultuous relationship with my family. I was miserable.

The days were long and the nights felt longer as the weeks slipped by. It was like I was sitting in the darkness, even when it was daytime, alone and invisible for all eternity. I was suffering under the weight of emotions I didn't understand. I still don't know how to express those feelings of emptiness even now. Does that make sense? Like there's some big, giant feeling inside of you that overwhelms every rational thought?

I knew that I wanted to be left alone, but at the same time, I could not bear the loneliness. I just wanted it to stop. Even when a friend negotiated a truce with this mate, I didn't go out. I stayed inside and let the darkness envelop me.

I was barely seventeen years old and had lost all hope and verve. As I knelt restlessly on my bed, I saw only two ways out of my misery. One was for someone, somewhere, to reach out and somehow save me, or two, to end my own life.

Yes. I was so low that I thought about suicide.

I had already considered how I would do it, but I didn't think I had the courage to carry it out. I *wanted* to do it. I desperately needed a way out of the darkness and something to soothe the excruciating knots in my stomach that were caused by my anxiety. I thought that suicide was the answer. All I knew was my pain was relentless. I would actually punch myself in the stomach and hit my head against the wall just to distract myself from the emotional agony. I was alone, and it seemed like nobody cared. Crying wasn't going to happen; I wasn't going to release my anxiety and depression through tears. After an argument with my father many months earlier, I swore that I would never cry again—a vow I intended to uphold.

I felt like I was in a deep hole without the knowledge, power, or energy to get out.

I was lost.

One morning as I lay on my bed, I heard the phone ring. It was my grandmother. She had heard of a Catholic youth group running a few meetings close to our house and called to see if Rachel would be interested in going. She hadn't bothered to ask me as she thought I wouldn't be interested.

She was wrong. I was interested. I saw my family getting on with their lives, and it reminded me of the happiness and freedom I once had. I knew I needed to get out of the darkness and back to a functional life. I had hit a wall, was entertaining suicidal thoughts, and recognized that if I did not get help quickly, I would not survive much longer. I was in despair, but I somehow recognized this. I don't really know how, but I recognized that I needed help. I saw this as my opportunity to find my way back to life. I mustered up all the energy I had left and asked Mum if I could go.

My mother could not believe her ears.

I attended the youth group meeting looking for some kind of escape from my anguish, but I do admit there was a part of me that was reluctant about the whole thing.

I sat there at the back, refusing to participate in the games—they just seemed so frivolous—but I listened very attentively to what was going on. I observed everything. I saw the joy and tranquillity in the eyes of the young people there, and it reminded me of my childhood: that beautiful idyllic dream that had once made me so happy. The music the group sang was lovely and gave me a sense of that idyllic peace. The youth group preacher also made an impact on me with his leadership and inspired words.

I did not quite understand what was going on in my mind and heart, but I wanted more of those sensations, more of the soothing peace instilled in me that day. I had every intention of going back the next week to experience it again, and I returned home feeling surprisingly hopeful.

I walked through the door to the curious glances of my parents and headed straight to my bedroom to think.

I thought about the meeting. Alone in my room, I reflected on what the preacher said about Jesus. It surprised me that he spoke about Jesus as though he knew him personally, like they were buddies or something. He said to the group that we too could talk to Jesus, and that if we did, Jesus would be interested in what we had to say. Well, I believed in God; after all, I came from a Catholic upbringing. But I hadn't thought that God would be interested in what I had to say or that he would also be willing to talk back to me. After all, God had bigger issues to deal with such as solving world poverty, helping refugees, and stopping wars. I was also convinced that he had more important people to communicate with than me. People like holy people and world leaders.

I surrender to you
Those dark, cold places

from the song
"I Surrender to You"

I decided to give it a try anyway. What did I have to lose?

I set the scene for a conversation with Jesus. I locked the door of my bedroom, sat on one of the chairs, and tapped the other saying, "Jesus, sit down. I want to talk to you!"

It felt awkward at first. I was, when I thought about it, talking to an empty chair. I tried to put those feelings aside. As strange as this might seem, and I know it must sound a bit weird, there was a monumental shift within me that day. I was, for just a few moments, able to believe that someone was listening to me, and it made all the difference. I felt a little bit of light come back into my heart, so I persevered with this strange little set up.

Every day for several weeks, I placed the chairs the same way. Two chairs facing each other. Every day I sat in one of those chairs for at least ten minutes and recounted my day, my feelings, and my desires to Jesus, whom I began to believe was sitting on the other chair. I also began to pray on a regular basis.

My general attitude was also improving, and I was leaving my room more often. I would catch my mother looking at me, as if trying to see into my heart. She wasn't blind to my situation and encouraged my interest in the youth group. I also made time to immerse myself in the water. We had a pool, but I started spending more time at the beach.

I returned to that youth meeting every Saturday night. My hope was growing and my pain was slowly withdrawing as I continued to pray every day. I lived each week to attend the next meeting; I suddenly had something to keep me going. The loneliness that was killing me slowly began to subside as my faith in God began to grow. I felt my self-destructive urges start to fade. At the meetings, I began to feel I was loved and liked by the other teenagers and leaders of the group, and it began to dawn on me that there was a God who was with me not only as I sat before him in my room but all throughout my day. God surrounded me, and as I surrendered to him, my life changed.

God chose to take this to a whole new level on Thursday the second of December, 1999. I am not one to remember dates, or any details like that at all, but I clearly remember that day and date. I returned home from a long day at school and prepared for my usual few minutes of fellowship with Jesus. I spoke to the apparently empty chair about my day. The monologue was quite mundane, and as I wound up, I sat quietly to listen to Jesus speak back. I didn't hear any response, which was no surprise. It's very rare, even today, that I hear God speak to me during times of prayer, but what prayer does is give me a sense of peace and a deep knowledge that God is with me throughout the course of my day. Up to that point, this was enough to keep me returning to prayer every day.

On that particular Thursday, something kept me waiting in silent prayer for longer than usual, and that's when God spoke back.

As I was sitting there in silence, I suddenly had a sense that there was somebody in the room with me. I did not see anything at first, but I just had a strange feeling that there was somebody there. It wasn't a scary or creepy feeling, like when the hair goes up on the back of your neck, nothing like that. I sat there, closed my eyes and after a short while opened them again. That is when I saw it. There was someone sitting in the chair in front of me. A gentle-looking person, a man. I recognized that it was Jesus.

As I gazed at him, my heart, out of nowhere, started to fill with anger. Of all things, *anger*! This feeling grew until I stood from my chair and started to point at the figure in my room. I had years of rage to let out and my heart needed healing.

It was like the Holy Spirit had chosen that moment to help me get rid of the inner fury, loneliness, and regret that was still left in my heart. I was ready to release all of my pain, and in order to take it from me, he needed to bring it to the surface.

I pointed hard, thrusting my finger at him. At first I bit my tongue, but then in a loud cry of anger, I asked, "Why did you abandon me? Why did you allow me to go through all that pain? Where were you when I wanted to die? If you are a loving God, then why did you allow me to go through so much anxiety and anger alone?"

I threw questions at him but got no answer.

At this point, I was overcome by my rage, a terrible anger that I did not know I had. I thought I had purged all of my feelings, that my self-disgust was gone, but there it was again, only this time it was being directed towards God. All of my life I was told that God is in control, that he is omnibenevolent (all-caring), omniscient (all-knowing), and omnipotent (all-powerful). I believed that in my mind, but my heart was unsure.

The anger I carried surprised me, and I had to wonder how deep the well was. Where did it all come from? How did I ever manage to store it for so long without exploding?

I poured out my rage to Jesus, letting it all out, letting it overflow. There was nothing hidden under the surface anymore. It was laid bare.

I looked back at Jesus sitting there on the chair, but this time I saw tears stream down his face. He was crying! This enraged me once again, and I jumped up and said in a loud voice, "Why are *you* crying? I should be the one crying, not you!"

But then it occurred to me that Jesus was not in tears because I was bullying him. He was not even upset that I was angry at him. No, the tears that he was crying were the tears I could not cry—the tears that I'd refused to cry many months previously after arguing with my father.

My heart broke.

They were the tears of my pain. I could see that he knew my heart and he understood my pain. He was perfectly aware of all my sin, my darkness, my mess, and my shame, and he loved me anyway. He loved me unconditionally, and for the first time in my life, I believed that beyond the shadow of a doubt. I understood that Jesus loved me in spite of my imperfections. I felt that my heart was about to explode with feelings of love.

I fell to my knees before that chair, broke the promise I had made to not cry again, and sobbed for every dark thought and every little bit of grief that filled my soul. My crying got louder and louder until I began to worry that my parents would hear me, so I grabbed a pillow and held it to my face to dampen the sound. I lay down before the chair, curled into the fetal position, and drowned in floods of tears for more than two hours. As I cried myself out, an overwhelming feeling of joy grew in my spirit. It felt like the beautiful weight of unconditional love. Jesus was healing my angry and lonely heart.

Through the tears I asked Jesus for forgiveness for all the sins of my life, and I begged him to take over those dark, cold places that I had not yet surrendered to him. I asked Jesus to be the true Lord and Savior of my life, and I committed to a relationship with him from that day on.

≈

Christianity is primarily seen by many as a *religion* rather than a *relationship*. Well, it isn't. A Christian does not follow a religion but a person: Jesus Christ. The purpose of the practices of religion (prayer, practice of the sacraments, and worship with the believing community) is to serve and deepen our relationship with God, personally and communally.

Even though I still had a lot to straighten out in my life after I committed to Jesus—such as getting rid of old habits, dealing with my addictions, and fixing errant behaviors—my life has never been the same since. Looking back, there were four things that led me out of that abyss:

- prayer,
- family,
- community, and
- professional medical help.

I knew I needed to get out of my dark mindset and find hope. I had prayed to hear God's voice on that day in 1999 and my prayers were answered in a profound way. I found my way back to faith and back to God.

It was the first of several turning points in my life. I was now surrounded by a community of believers who would be patient with my ongoing addictions and help me through to complete freedom, and my relationship with my parents was improving every day. I found hope in the glimmerings of a personal *relationship* with Jesus Christ, the risen Son of God. Having a relationship with him was redemptive. From the darkness, I could see a future, whereas a few months before that I had been hopeless, anxious, and with nowhere to turn. I discovered this loving relationship with Christ, and it was like standing on the shoulders of a giant. And if it could happen for me, it could happen for anyone.

We were created for a relationship. God designed us that way. We were not designed to live and flourish alone. Human beings are social beings, and we thrive as we relate to the world around us: to things in nature, animals, other human beings, and God. We are the only beings on this earth that can have a personal relationship with God. The rest of creation can relate to God indirectly as they do what God has created them to do, but only human beings can know the heart and mind of God.

The sad thing is that too many Christians don't know this. Until I had the encounter with Jesus Christ in my room that Thursday afternoon, I really did not know what it meant to have a personal relationship with God. I knew about God. I liked and loved God, but I had never personally encountered him.

Look at it this way. A few months ago, I went on holiday to Far North Queensland with my late friend, Fr. Chris Reay. It was to be our last holiday together, as he was severely weakened by a cancer spreading throughout his body. On one particular morning, I needed some time alone so I took a walk to the local parish church to attend Sunday morning Mass. I was welcomed by the usher at the door who recognized that I was not from the area. She asked where I was from.

"I'm from Bendigo in Victoria," I said.

She quickly responded, "Wow! I've heard of Bendigo. That's where Fr. Rob Galea is from. Do you know him?"

I looked at her awkwardly, wondering if it was some kind of joke, but she waited patiently for an answer. "Actually, yes, I do know him," I responded. I took my parish bulletin and quickly walked away before she realized who I was and it caused her embarrassment.

I sat there in the back pew wondering about what had just happened. She knew *about* me, but she obviously did not know me personally. I was standing right before her and she did not recognise me. It occurred to me during that Mass that this is what it is like for so many Christians. We know so much about Jesus. We know his words, the things he did, the things we should avoid and do to please him, but do we know him personally? Would we recognise him if he stood before us face-to-face?

> He was in the world, and the world was made through him, yet the world did not know him. He came to his own, and his own people did not receive him. But to all

who did receive him, who believed in his name, he gave
the right to become children of God, who were born, not
of blood nor of the will of the flesh nor of the will of man,
but of God. (Jn 1:10–13, ESV)

God walked this earth more than two thousand years
ago so that we could know him personally. Through his
Holy Spirit you can still do this today. You do not need to
have a supernatural audience with God like I did in order
to have a relationship with God. What I experienced was
extraordinary, but in reality, my relationship with God
today is quite ordinary. I speak and listen to God every day.
He is part of my everyday life. Through getting to know
Jesus, I have learned to love him and now have no greater
desire than to honor him and become like him.

I speak to God as I wake up in the morning. "Good
morning, Jesus," I say, then I lie still and imagine him giving
me a hug. As I look for a place to park my car, I say, "Jesus,
please help me find a parking space." As I lift heavy weights
on the bench press at the gym, I pray, "Jesus, please don't
let me drop this weight and kill myself." When I get scared
before a speaking engagement, I stand still and remember
that Jesus walks with me onto every stage, in every meeting.
When I stop at a traffic light, I watch the people crossing
the road. When I see a beautiful woman, a happy child, or
a joyful family, I smile, look to Jesus, and say, "Jesus, good
work!" I see Jesus smile back at me.

I speak to God, but I don't necessarily hear an audible
voice speak back to me. All I get is a deep understanding
and knowledge that God stands beside me, giving me the
strength and joy to face each day. He loves me, he likes me,
and he is involved in my biggest life events and the most
trivial of thoughts and activities.

God loves you more than you could ever know. He knows your joy and fully understands your pain. God is able to take that darkness in your life, that *mess*, and turn it into a beautiful *message*, but he can only do that when we hand all things over to him, when we surrender our hearts, lives, burdens, and pain. God created you for joy, freedom and life. He says in John 10:10, "I have come that they may have life, and have it to the full."

This freedom is yours if you are willing to allow God into your life. Pray this prayer with me:

> Lord Jesus, I come before you, just as I am. I am sorry for my sins, I repent of my sins, please forgive me. In your name, I forgive all others for what they have done against me. I surrender my pain, anger, loneliness, shame, and brokenness. You know the dark, cold places in my heart; here they are, Lord. Take them from me. Help me carry the cross that I sometimes find unbearable. I give you my entire self, Lord Jesus, and ask that you let me know you personally and love you selflessly. Heal me, change me, and strengthen me in body, soul, and spirit.
>
> Come Lord Jesus, cover me with your precious blood, and fill me with your Holy Spirit. I thank you, Jesus, and I shall follow you every day of my life. Amen.
>
> Mary, my mother, Queen of Peace, all the angels and saints, please help me. Amen.

And once you have prayed, knowing that God welcomes you with open arms, here are a few simple things you can do to grow in your relationship with God.

1. TALK TO GOD. Make some time every day to speak to God and to actively listen to him. Pray. If it helps, set up two chairs and sit in one of them. Imagine God's Holy Spirit sitting in the chair in front of you. Tell him about what is on your mind and heart. He cares. Then stop, be still, listen. Let him embrace you

2. **DUST OFF YOUR BIBLE AND READ IT.** God's Word is his love letter to you. This is one way God will speak to you. Ask him to inspire you as you read Matthew, Mark, Luke, and John. Imagine yourself as one of the characters in the Bible watching Jesus speak, act, and proclaim his Word. Read through the psalms and make King David's prayers your prayers. Imagine St. Paul instructing you through his letters to the Romans and Galatians. "Your word is a lamp for my feet, a light on my path" (Ps 119:105).

3. **SACRAMENTS.** Watch God work in and through you as you participate in the sacraments. He nourishes you through the Eucharist, forgives your sins, and reconciles you with him and his Body, the Church, as you receive the Sacrament of Reconciliation. He heals your body and soul through the Sacrament of the Anointing of the Sick. Sacraments are signs of God's living presence among us.

4. **COMMUNITY.** Find a community of faith that can encourage you in your journey towards getting to know, love, and serve God. You were not created to walk alone. You need other pilgrims to help you "press on toward the goal to win the prize for which God has called [you] heavenward in Christ Jesus" (Phil 3:14).

Playing the guitar helped me to connect with God in new ways.

TWO

Part of the Group

The winter months pass quickly in Malta as summer is always lurking around the corner. Just as the bougainvillea stretches to meet the sun and burst into its beautiful array of colors, so was my life beginning to take a very definite course, nourished by the warmth of a life-giving, loving God.

In just a few weeks my life had changed dramatically. I had a new sense of purpose and there was a new depth of joy and hope in my heart, which I hadn't known previously. My purpose was to know God more, to try and love him more perfectly and to serve him in whatever way I could. As this inward change began to happen, those around me also noticed a change in me.

One evening after the youth group, my parents came to pick me up. My brother, Joseph, was with them and all the way home I couldn't stop speaking about Jesus and his love for me. My mother was in the front seat in tears, as she knew my struggles and how God had touched my life. As someone who is close to God herself, she understood better than anyone. My dad was silent, but probably wondering how long this phase would last, and Joseph turned to me and said, "Rob, I wish you were like this all the time."

That statement hit me hard. His words said much that was unsaid. For the first time in a long time, he didn't see me as an annoying, bullying and cynical person. His eyes were being opened to a new reality, one in which my peace led to peace for him, something which would hopefully last for both of us.

Rachel, Daniel, and my other school friends also noticed the change—more than I did actually. Daniel often asked me how I grew to be so at peace with myself so quickly. And over the following weeks, it wasn't just Daniel asking that question—I also got asked by several of my school friends why I was so happy all the time. I could not wipe the smile off my face. I was at peace for the first time in a long time, and when I acknowledged that I had experienced God's love, I was left with comments like, "Does that mean you are going to become a priest?"

I quickly responded that there was no way on earth that I would ever become a priest!

≈

Draw me to your presence
Oh Lord

from the song
"Draw Me"

Growing in the love and knowledge of Jesus is not like getting close to a great magician, who changes everything with a swipe of his hand. On the contrary, it is a lifelong journey where decisions have to be made on a daily basis so that we can learn to overcome the things that hinder us from growing as better Christians. I still had a lot of pain to heal, my depression and anxiety still required treatment, and there were many broken relationships that needed mending. I had my addictions that I was yet to truly face and overcome, but I was not alone. Now I could face all these situations in the knowledge that I had a companion who cared so much for and about me, one who would never walk away from me, and who would never ask me to do anything that would harm me or those I loved.

And so, for the most part, my bad habits began to lose their hold on me. I no longer felt the need to lie or steal or cheat. Once I changed my environment and surrounded myself with godly and good people, I began to learn more about self-control and accountability. I believed that I owed it to those who cared for me to respect their trust in me. Slowly but surely, with such new friends, I began to lose my need to smoke and take drugs. It wasn't always easy; I had days where I craved nicotine in particular, but I persevered. My sobriety was worth it.

One of the areas that I found very challenging was controlling my temper, especially if I became agitated with my friends. I had developed a nasty habit of immediately giving into my feelings and lashing out whenever I felt slighted. For instance, if I was angry at someone I wouldn't think twice about throwing the first thing I could grab at them or saying something horribly mean with the intention of hurting their feelings. Yeah. Not cool. I had to learn that with God by my side, I had the power to control my impulses; I needed to learn to be positive in my conversations about and with them. I had to remember how to care about others. The reactions of Rachel and Joseph towards my behavior were my first reminder of this, and the youth group reinforced it.

I wanted to be free from any ties that held me away from the joy I was now experiencing. The cigarettes, the drugs, the stealing, the lies, and the addiction to sex and pornography all had to go. For a while, the desire for anything but God disappeared, and it was easy to live free from all of those compulsions, but as the months went by and the demons of my past began to visit me again, I knew that I had to come clean about my past with those I could trust. I realized that I needed the support of the community and even some professional guidance to help me manage my addictions. Even though I had found the strength to overcome some powerful cravings to that point, I knew that I would not be able to resist them forever, so I spoke about my past addictions and current temptations with my senior youth leader. With his help, and the support of an encouraging community and a lot of prayer, I began to find the spiritual and mental muscle to break those chains once and for all. My youth leader also encouraged me to go and see a medical doctor, which was a crucial part of my recovery. I had stopped taking care of my health while I indulged myself, and I was now paying for it. Going to the doctor actually felt like hitting the reset button; my new run at health started on that day. I didn't need medication for my depression, but the doctor suggested that I look after my physical health by exercising and improving my diet. This helped me improve my mental health.

The temptation to revisit these "old friends" often reappeared while in recovery and still visits me on occasion today, but having built a good understanding of the power of belief I have in Jesus, the support of a believing community, the availability of professional help, and the grace and mercy found in the sacraments—particularly in the Sacrament of Reconciliation and the Eucharist—I walk confidently towards a life of holy freedom.

My relationship with my parents was also improving as I began to love and accept myself, and not blame them for everything that I was not happy about in my own life. As I began to pray, meditate and think about my life in the recent past, I started to recognise my lack of patience and my aggression towards my parents. I made a conscious decision to listen more and appreciate all they had done and continued to do for me. As a result, I was able to open my heart to my mother, and encouragingly, I was able to have long and good conversations with my father. Even though Dad and I still disagreed on many things, they very rarely ended in angry arguments as they had done, almost without fail, in the past. On the rare occasion where tempers rose, my mother would quickly step in and remind me to let go and forgive. Family time became something I cherished.

My hunger for God was growing all the time. I sought God as much as I could. I would take refuge in my room where I would pray, sing songs of praise, pour out my heart to God, and then sit and listen and wait for him to fill my heart. I was totally immersed in the loving presence of God. When I finished my quiet time, I would sit and journal, writing about his involvement in my day and in my prayers. Some days I would write letters to God and then be still and listen to God writing back to me. I would write down what I would imagine him saying. These journals, which I still own, have survived as a testament to those days and nights when God became a real Father to me, and I came to know Jesus as my brother.

I want to share a couple of entries with you now. In talking to Jesus, I was able to let go of the burdens of my soul. I became free through my writing, this other form of communion. I find that keeping a prayer journal has great power and would highly recommend that you consider keeping a journal too. It serves as a map of your journey with God, as well as a means to focus on days when prayer seems like nothing but a struggle. Here is a sneak-peak at my journey right at the very beginning of my walk with God.

An Excerpt from Wednesday, February 2, 2000

My precious Jesus, sometimes I wonder whether to ask you to show me less of your love. I want to be loved by you and I want to feel your love more than anything else, but at times my heart feels like it is going to burst; it feels like if you love me any more I would just die. I suppose that is what heaven is like, isn't it? It's this constant and eternal love-embrace of Daddy God that our bodies just cannot handle here on earth. I can't wait for heaven! I can't wait for that embrace! Keep me faithful to you so that I may bask in your love forever. I love you!

An Excerpt from Sunday, November 5, 2000

Jesus, it is soon my birthday. I am amazed how much has changed since my last birthday. You are drawing me closer to your powerful, gentle and merciful light. My greatest joy, Jesus, is that you have been with me all along and will continue to be. You are so patient with me. I would have given up on myself ages ago, but you never will. You are my best friend, my brother and my Lord. For this birthday, Jesus, please give me another year of fellowship with you. I want to be a saint; I want to be just like you. I am so far away from that right now, but with you by my side I can be the saint you have called me to be. I love you, Jesus, and there is nothing I want more than to love you more!

It's intimate, I know, but a relationship with Jesus is just that.

My spiritual and personal growth continued every day, and my relationship with Jesus intensified as I made my mother accompany me to Mass every evening after school. She indulged me, even though I know that on some days she had already been to Mass earlier that morning. I was so full of my love for Jesus that I needed to express it, and I knew that there was no closer connection to him than through the Eucharist.

I continued to grow in my faith, and sought out someone who would become my new spiritual companion,
journeying with me through the next stage of my faith journey. My mother continued to accompany me in my faith,
but I needed someone outside of my own household too. I
wanted to expand my community.

It was at this time I met Fr. Joe Borg, an elderly Jesuit
priest. He became my *spiritual director*, a person who would
help me unpack and make sense of what I had experienced
spiritually over the previous few weeks. Every month I
would take the bus to go and visit him in Valletta.

It was through my regular meetings with him that I met
God the Father in the unique healing of the Sacrament of
Reconciliation. We would sit down in the church and talk;
sometimes for hours. I would tell him where I was with God
and mention the times I had failed to be faithful to him. I
would always leave with an overwhelming sense of joy
after Fr. Joe prayed for me, offered me Christ's forgiveness
on behalf of the Church, and encouraged me on my spiritual
journey. Even today I find the Sacrament of Reconciliation
one of the most healing and encouraging sacraments.

This sacrament is sometimes known as Penance or
Confession, but I personally think it is best termed as the
Sacrament of Reconciliation because it reminds me of what
God does through the sacrament and not about what we
are required to do. The truth is, God has intended a perfect
union between himself and us, but we reject this fellowship
every time we sin. Sure, we need to be sorry for what we
have done, and we do need to confess our sins as the scripture says (see James 5:16 and 1 John 1:9), but the extraordinary sign of this sacrament is that God the Father runs
towards us with open and forgiving arms as we turn back
to him, and through this embrace offered to us by the priest,
he reconciles us back to himself and his Church.

Every time I met with Fr. Joe, I would show up with a list of all of my sins and read the list out to him during my conversation with him. I wanted to be pure and without sin; anxious not to leave out anything that might have remotely offended God throughout the month, so my list was always comprehensive. I love how patient Fr. Joe was with me during this time. He gently weaned me off the list and taught me to see the sacrament as an embrace of God the Father. Like the prodigal son who approached his father with rehearsed words, the father ran towards the son and put a ring on his finger, welcoming him home, stopping the son mid-sentence (see Luke 15:11–32). Words did not matter; what mattered was that the sorrow and repentance of the son was met by the disproportionate mercy of the Father. That was such a revelation for me.

I use this sacrament regularly and am so often overwhelmed at how God the Father continues to run towards me with his warm embrace, no matter how far I wander.

≈

If you had told me in the months before my transformation that I would be going to church regularly for the Sacrament of Reconciliation and to a youth group, I would have run a mile. Now I look forward to the soothing forgiveness of Jesus in this sacrament. I really needed healing in my life and this was one sure way of it happening. The grace to open one's life before the Lord and to receive his healing forgiveness is really beyond our comprehension, and yet in the Gospels, Jesus always helps people to realize their dignity as full human beings—the blind Bartimeus, the woman caught in adultery, the woman at the well, Zacchaeus, the apostles themselves, and even a repentant thief. I saw my life mirrored in so many of them, and yet I was learning that I too was precious in the eyes of God.

However, much as I loved my time with Fr. Joe, the highlight of my week was always the youth meeting. I couldn't wait to join in the praise and worship, or listen to Sue, our joyful and charismatic leader, break open the Word of God and share it with us. It was the sense of *belonging* that really resonated with me and began to prepare me for future days.

Everyone has an innate desire to belong to another and I found my belonging among people who thought like me, who desired the same thing. In my case, it was to get to know Jesus Christ intimately.

Ten weeks earlier I had been a prisoner in my room, wrapped in self-loathing, guilt, and isolation. Now, here I was, free of such shackles. Instead of wanting to die, I wanted to live in Jesus' presence. I found myself less concerned about my own needs and wants, but I had a new excitement for life and a longing to share this newfound unconditional love and freedom with others. It was as though I had discovered a great treasure that I needed to tell the world about.

But those honeymoon days of revelling in God's loving presence would soon be put to the test. It's always the way. And just as I thought everything was going right for me . . .

It was in January, 2000. One night at our weekly youth meeting, we received the terrible news that our gatherings would soon stop. The youth group was only a temporary group and the leaders needed to return to their work and their own prayer groups. We were to find our own way, armed with what we had learned and had been given in our meetings.

My world started to crumble as I saw all my support systems falling down, dismantled in one single announcement, and my fears began to gnaw at me once again. How was I supposed to continue without the support of the group? I *needed* to belong. I needed the support of like-minded people. I needed to know that there were others there to support me in my quest to come closer to Jesus and live a better life.

I had only just found my way out of the dark, and here it was, claiming me yet again.

Slowly, it began to dawn on me that although my relationship with God was paramount, I also needed the loving support of a Christian community to encourage me and walk with me on my journey. I hoped that they needed me too, as together we built up the body of Christ.

St. Paul, in his letter to the Corinthians, describes the Church as the Body of Christ. You and I, he says, are particular parts of that body. Some are the hands, others the feet. Some are the eyes and others the ears. We all need each other to function properly, and together we are all dependent on Christ, the head of the body. The eye cannot say to the hand, "I don't need you!" and the head cannot say to the feet, "I don't need you!" (see 1 Corinthians 12:12–27).

I knew that I could not survive alone. I was enthusiastic to continue this new path of holiness, but I also knew that I was weak and could easily fall back into my old lifestyle, addictions and depression.

The cure for my ailments was the support of a community who would answer my many questions, be patient with my weaknesses, and give me the courage to do what was needed if I was to become whole and healed again and give my life to Jesus. It was clear to me that I needed to find a new group. I had to reach outside of my safe circle and find a community that loved Jesus like I did.

≈

When I think of this period in my life, I am reminded of the stories from the Gospel of Mark (see Mark 2:1–12), and the evangelist who told the story of five friends. One of the

five was completely broken and hopeless. He was an out-
cast and useless in the eyes of the world. The friends looked
beyond his weakness and saw his potential. They knew of
one person alone who could help him live up to that potential, and they did whatever it took to carry him there. They
made their way through crowds and did not stop when the
door to Jesus was seemingly closed. They climbed onto a
rooftop, carrying the full weight of their friend with them,
and tore through the roof to deliver their friend to the feet
and healing hands of God.

This is what the believing community had been for me,
and now I had to make sure that this would continue not
just for me but so that I too could reach out to others in
need, if and when I was asked. By this time, I was really
understanding the power of community and how giving
and receiving went together. I was thriving in that sort of
environment.

The hunt was on for a new group. I inquired among
my peers about other such groups in the area, and with
my friend Mark, who attended the youth group for the ten
weeks I was there, we set about trying to find a supportive
and caring group. My mother also made some calls and
managed to get us to a meeting at the Marana Thà Community, a covenant Catholic community led by medical doctor
and faith healer Dr. John Bonnici Mallia.

In Marana Thà (which is the Greek word Μαραναθα,
translated as "come, Lord Jesus"), I found a welcoming
community. I was very happy there, feeling at ease among
both the young and old who took me under their wing in
those early days.

Within this new group I found support and good
examples of true followers of Christ. The people within the
community taught and showed me the value in the habit of
prayer, studying the Bible and the teachings of the Church,

and giving time and priority to my family. As a result, my improving relationships with my mother, father, brother, and sister began to flourish, and that provided me with more stability in my own life.

Dr. John himself was particularly supportive; he became my mentor, my role model, and spiritual father figure. When I found it difficult to believe in myself, he encouraged me to keep looking to Jesus, as he did, to help me to overcome my self-doubt and low self-esteem. What Dr. John was basically teaching me about was trust. I was learning to trust in God's great love for me, and so as a consequence, little by little, I was beginning to trust and believe more in myself.

I spent a lot of time with Dr. John. For a while, I wanted to become a doctor just like him. I wanted to travel around the world with him and spend my days learning from him, asking questions about God and about the faith. He was very patient with me and helped me become a better and more confident man. He helped me see Jesus in everyday life, and for this, I will be grateful for all of my days.

It was in the Marana Thà community that I began to understand and participate in the sacraments in a more meaningful way. Each sacrament held the key to the door of understanding God who reveals his love to us, and I was beginning to see this.

It was here that I also learned to play music. It seems strange to me now that I'd come this far along my journey without it. Music would become the key to my healing and much later, one of my primary tools in which I could bring the love of God to others, though I did not realize it at the time. The Marana Thà group needed someone to play in the worship band, and Andrew, the leader of the band, asked if I was interested in attempting to play the guitar. I went home that day with a guitar and asked my mother to teach me a few chords. She herself played the guitar and sang in her own weekly prayer group, so she was a reliable teacher while I was just beginning. I would practice every day under her watchful guidance, but I also had my own influences, such as the guitarists on MTV. I would copy their chord progressions and try to mimic them. I spent hours working at this craft. The guitar was soon like an extra limb, and we were quickly inseparable.

Music is a powerful thing. Music changes hearts; it changes people. It is a language that transcends the mind, culture, age, and language. At times when I could not deal with life's circumstances, at times of loneliness and change, music was always there for me. After an argument with my parents, I would feel isolated after slamming my bedroom door behind me, at least I did until I played my favorite record and then I felt comforted and consoled. In moments of joy, turning to God with music let my soul soar like an eagle. St. Augustine was reported to have said that when we sing, we pray twice: once in the words we address to God and again in singing the melody which lifts the soul towards God in a way which words fail to do. That just feels so right.

Playing and creating music allowed me to connect with God in ways I never imagined possible. I would spend hours with a guitar in my hands singing psalms, hymns, and spiritual songs to my audience of one, praising him for his goodness in my life and crying out to him for mercy for the world, my friends, and myself. Later, when I began to play in public, I began to see and hear of others experiencing this same profound connection I had with God. I was so happy to be able to contribute to the community in this way.

Soon I was good enough to begin playing in the band. As my musical skills began to develop and improve, I began to travel with the community and was privileged to go to many places around and outside of Malta as a member of the band. While Dr. John gave lectures and teachings, we would play and provide the music for healing services and other liturgical events. My repertoire wasn't vast, but what I knew I played well.

I have never been comfortable in front of a crowd, but Dr. John pushed me to speak and sing in public. It was with this community that I began learning to overcome my fear and be my authentic self on stage, although it took some time. I also learned to serve others through Dr. John. As I travelled with him, I learned not to seek any attention for myself but sought to support him and his ministry. Sometimes the only thing I would do is carry his bags and make sure he was looked after. He was almost sixty years old at the time.

These were days that God was using to prepare me for what was to come next.

When God comes into a life, he is always faithful to bring to completion the good work he began in that soul, heart, mind, and body (see Philippians 1:6). God's grace continued to work through my life, as with the support of a believing community, I continued to grow and hear his voice deep within.

Secretly, oh so secretly, I had begun to wrestle with the fact that perhaps the Lord was calling me to serve him in a more direct way in ministry, in the priesthood. My abiding love for Jesus was consuming me, and I'd already come to the conclusion that he was going to be in my life until the day I died. I was trying to figure out the best way to respond to that and to reconcile doubts that were hindering my commitment.

This was a far cry from the guy who had wrestled with suicide, addictions, and self-loathing.

I was strongly considering the possibility of responding to what I believed to be God's call, but thankfully I did not need to make my mind up just yet. There was plenty more life to be lived first!

≋

I was thoroughly enjoying my relationship with God. It was giving me a new joy and hope for the future. I could not wait to see what God could do with my life if I continued to live it by his side. However, I knew that it would not be easy. There was so much to distract me from the spiritual life. My studies, exercises, and music as well as hanging out with friends and the temptation to conform to the expectations of the world around me held me back. The more I thought about it, the more I began to realize that walking with Jesus was countercultural. I wanted to be a man of faith in a world that claims there is and can be no God. I wanted to spend the rest of my life growing in love with God, but I knew even then that this could not happen without a commitment to a faith community and to prayer. Faith is a gift, and I felt so grateful for it that I wanted, like the good steward (see Matthew 25:14–30), to make the most out of it.

I was determined to stay connected to the Church that I felt society was beginning to lose confidence in and gradually despise. I wanted to be pure and a person of integrity when the media and culture were considering chastity and integrity as oppressive and impossible.

I was committed to attending and serving at my weekly youth group and at daily Mass in my local parish, but I also put a lot of energy into developing a habit of daily structured and ongoing conversation with God. Just like in any committed relationship, we get busy and distracted and sometimes fail to make the time to give our undivided attention to that other person in our lives. I always loved how my dad would call Mum from work a few times a day to see how she was doing. There was nothing possessive or intense about these calls—they were just so connected and he missed her. This showed me that he was thinking of her throughout his day and not only when he was home. It showed me the power of a healthy relationship, a loving relationship. I wanted the same thing with God.

I committed to one hour of quiet time with God every day. After school I would head to my room, lock the door, play some praise and worship music, speak and listen to God, and then write in my journal. Some days it was easy and other days it was torturous, but I stuck to it. I disciplined myself to fall to my knees and be generous with God on a daily basis. Every day I would find peace in the very spot where just a few months earlier, I had painfully cried myself to sleep, hoping that I would never wake up. Making time to be with God allowed me to be more aware of God's presence throughout my day (see 1 Thessalonians 5:17).

My prayers never ended in my room. As I did my homework I became aware that God studied with me. When I went out with my friends or went to school, I knew he was there. I woke up every morning smiling because I was aware of his presence. The days I got too busy to offer myself to God in prayer and stillness, my practice of experiencing the presence of God throughout my day also suffered.

Committing to spend time with God every day not only helped me maintain my relationship with God but it was also a means to know and understand his heart and will.

I wanted nothing more than to serve God. But what did he want me to do? I knew that God knows all things and had a purpose for my life. He could not have brought me this far and not have big plans for my future. I was excited and could not wait to see what God could do with my willing heart.

I spoke to God about my future daily. "Jesus. What do you want for my life? What plans do you have for me? I want to serve you and do not want to miss out on anything you have in store for me."

I prayed, I listened, I journaled, and I spoke to my spiritual directors, Fr. Joe and Dr. John. For a long time I heard nothing and felt nothing. I was left with this burning heart, not knowing what to do and where to go with it. As I waited, for months and years, I just had to trust that God was in control. He would eventually reveal where I was to go with my desire to serve.

In hindsight, I can understand that God still had a lot of work to do in my heart before he could reveal the extent of his plans for my life. If he had told me back then that I would eventually become a priest, work in youth ministry, and move to Australia, I would have probably run away from him!

God rarely reveals the full extent of his plans for our lives at once, but he slowly melts and moulds our hearts to be able to surrender to the next step which he reveals in time. One gradual—often blind—step at a time. I would occasionally look back and be in awe at where he had brought me.

"But *how* can we be shown God's will?" I can almost hear you ask. I get asked that question all the time.

It's often in quite ordinary ways. Through listening to God in prayer, meditating on his Word, speaking to God, and surrendering your heart every day. Staying close to the community—the Church community—helps us discern God's will.

In my case, people began seeing things in me that I did not see in myself.

"You will be a good worship leader, why don't you try learning to play the guitar?"

"Have you ever considered the priesthood?"

"We need some help with filming, will you please help out?"

I would take all that I heard in prayer to my spiritual director, either Fr. Joe or Dr. John, to see where this fitted in my life. I also journaled as I went along. Looking back at previous posts in my journal, I could see a map from where God had brought me and where he was leading me.

My family, too, had a big part in helping me discern God's will for my life. My mother in particular. She prayed for me constantly, right from the very beginning. Even when my behavior was going from bad to worse, she did not give up. She never lost faith in her child. When I felt defeated and alone she knew one day I would walk free, away from hopelessness and become instead an instrument of hope for others. She believed because of her trust in God. She believed in a God of miracles. I, who was broken, would one day reach out to the broken.

My mother became my closest spiritual companion. We would talk for hours about what God had been telling each of us in our own prayer times as well as the dreams and hopes in our hearts. One of those dreams was that we would one day share a stage and preach together. It has not happened yet, but I still live in hope that we will see that come to pass. In times of struggle and doubt Mum was and is my greatest encouragement; she always reminds me to turn back to God. I recall with a deep feeling of consolation the times she would come to my room and pray over me when she sensed I was feeling a bit down. She would sit on my bed, speaking to Jesus out loud and stroking my hair as I lay on my bed, deep in my darkness and grief.

Mum has a beautiful gift of knowledge (see 1 Corinthians 12:8). As she sat there praying for me, she would often see and hear things about me in her spirit. She would then address her prayer according to what she was seeing or hearing. I knew that this was God revealing these things to her, as there was no way she could know some of the things she was speaking out loud. This would often bring me to tears and on more than one occasion I would beg Jesus to stop showing her things just in case she saw more than I was comfortable with her seeing. It is difficult to understand how broken I really was, and yet in my deep melancholy and depression, she saw the Lord coming and releasing me from this.

I was (and still am) far from perfect, but she knew that I was working towards the best version of me. Every time she prayed I was left encouraged and with a deep sense of joy and peace.

"I saw a picture," she said to me one day, well before the phone call from my grandmother that led me to the youth group and eventually Dr. John. "In this picture, you were sitting down in a circle with some young people, you had a guitar in your hands, and they were listening to you sing."

I was attentive to what she said, but it didn't make sense to me as I didn't know how to play the guitar and I had never sung in front of anyone before. I was shy, lacking in self-confidence, and feeling worthless, so this just didn't make sense to me.

"One more thing," she added, "in this picture you were wearing a black shirt with a priest's white collar."

I felt fury rise within me as I stood up from the chair, pushed it away, and stormed off angrily, shouting a few colorful words at my mother as I headed back to my room, slamming the door shut behind me.

How dare she impose her dreams on me! Me? A priest! I did not want to become a priest! I wanted to get married, and besides, I wasn't even sure I believed in God.

That little tantrum came long before I found my faith. In hindsight, I can see that God did speak to her through that image. Today I hold it as a confirmation of God's miraculous grace in my life. However, back then that was a word spoken to my mother's heart by God to encourage her not to give up and to keep praying for her deeply troubled son. Through that she was able to attain a deep vision of what I could be and that my darkness and imprisonment then would not define my future.

One of the keys to persisting in prayer is the gift of vision. Vision is catching a glance or a glimpse of what God is capable of and knowing that our current hopeless situation does not have the final word but that our loving, faithful God does. Think on the story of the persistent widow in Luke 18:1–8 who begged the judge for justice. She stopped at nothing and cried out to him day and night until she got what she needed because she knew the judge could deliver; she also understood that there was more to her future than living in the injustice that she was currently in.

I pray that you will be happy
That your smile will last forever

from the song
"Angel"

My mother prayed and trusted. She begged God to deliver me from the bondage that I was living in, and God heard her cries.

When I was crying myself to sleep at night, she was there. When I wished that my life would end, she was praying that I would find a new life. When I was overcome with melancholy and sadness she continued to pray that God would release me from this prison. In my mind, nobody cared, nobody knew my tears, nobody would miss me if I was gone. In her mind, she cared so much that she cried tears for me and longed for me to find new life and hope. I had no idea that as I cried in my room at night, my mother would be standing outside my bedroom door, listening to me cry, and praying for me. One day, she told me that she fell to her knees and told God that she would not get back up until he took me into his arms and saved me. She knelt there in tears, begging God for mercy and asking for Mother Mary to be my mother and carry me to Jesus. As she cried in her desperation, the Holy Spirit revealed to her that vision of me wearing a collar, holding the guitar, and surrounded by many young people. She knew then that it would be fulfilled. Her only charge was to keep praying until it did happen. If you think back to the day of the first youth group meeting, this was why my mother's joy was so complete in the car when I could not stop talking about Jesus.

It's worth noting that her prayer was not answered immediately. She prayed for a long time. At times, she wanted to give up; at other times she doubted what she had seen that night. When she could not carry the burden of prayer alone, she called family and friends to join her in prayer. They interceded, they fasted, and they trusted that I would somehow reach out to God's hand that was already held out towards me.

I am so grateful for my mother, for her vision and her persistence in prayer. I know I sit here writing this book and stand in front of thousands of teenagers every year, speaking and singing about the love of Jesus as an ordained Catholic priest, because of my mother's unwavering prayer. She truly is my hero.

≋

I know that there are mothers and fathers reading this book that have been praying for their children. Some of you can testify to God's grace through answered prayer, while others have been praying but don't know why God has not yet answered your plea. Maybe it is not children you are praying for: maybe you are the child or young adult being prayed for; maybe you are praying for friends, your parents, your girlfriend or boyfriend, your husband or wife, or for a situation to change in your own life.

Whatever your circumstances, I want to encourage you to persevere in your prayer and trust that God will have the final and triumphant word.

My counsel to you is to spend time with God, putting on his mind (see Philippians 2:5) and capturing his vision for your situation. God wants you to be free from anything that is holding you or others from him. This vision will give you the strength to stand firm in prayer until God's will is fulfilled (see Proverbs 29:18). Let God show you your situation through his eyes, and then, once you have grasped God's view, stop at nothing until you see God fulfill his promise. Bear in mind that God's ways are not our ways (see Isaiah 55:8–9), and if we entrust the situation to him, he will use whatever outcome for his good and your good too (see Romans 8:28). Remember, God's timing is not our timing (see 2 Peter 3:8).

Persistent prayer changes things. God doesn't need our prayer to accomplish his will, but for some reason, God chooses to use our prayer to bring about his purpose in this world. All throughout the Bible there are commands to pray, and this is because prayer ultimately does not change God but it does change us. Turning to God in prayer teaches us to trust God and to understand that he is in control.

I try to spend an hour in quiet prayer every day. Wherever I go, there are three things that I never compromise:

1. **Daily exercise**. The moment I land anywhere I head straight to the gym.
2. **Diet**. I try to eat clean 80 percent of the time and allow myself to "cheat" the rest of the 20 percent.
3. **Prayer**. I look for the closest church in the area and research the Mass times. I also keep my Bible and prayer journal with me.

I do not *find* the time for these three things; I *make* the time. Sometimes I have to wake up earlier to pray; other times I switch off the radio in my car and pray on my way to my next appointment. I remember my mother praying as she washed the dishes and did chores around the house. However, I do make an extra effort to have some distraction-free quiet time in prayer every day in my sacred space (usually a chapel, church, or sometimes my hotel room if I'm travelling). I don't think I would be able to do half the things I do if I did not pray daily. Prayer opens my eyes to see God with me at every moment of every day. Daily prayer requires discipline and support.

As an aside, have you ever tried going on a diet or decided to start exercising? I have. I started an exercise and clean diet routine a couple of months ago (not for the first time, sadly). I was very enthusiastic and determined and had planned my daily exercises. And every Sunday I would prepare my meals for the week. Looking good, right?

One evening after a big day in the parish, I headed down to the kitchen to eat my prepared high-protein, low-carb meal when I saw it: *temptation*. A generous parishioner had left a beautiful, shiny chocolate cake in our presbytery fridge.

Chocolate is my weakness. I'm sure some of you can relate. I can eat a whole large tub of Nutella in one sitting and still have room for a large block of chocolate.

I had been eating and exercising well to this point, so I quickly grabbed my meal and shut the fridge. As I ate my meal of chicken, broccoli, and quinoa, that chocolate cake kept coming to my mind. However, I finished my meal, washed my plate and got ready to go to the gym.

And then I lost control.

I walked back to the fridge just to see the kind of chocolate on the cake: Was it milk chocolate? Dark? I closed the fridge again, walked away, and without thinking, came straight back to the fridge. It was like my legs did it by themselves. I stared at the cake. One slice. What harm could that do? I had lost a good amount of weight and was going to the gym soon. Surely, I could afford one slice.

I grabbed a knife from the drawer and cut one generous slice. That slice was too large, I thought, so I cut another smaller slice. I ate that. My tastebuds were having a feast. One more small slice . . . and before I knew it, the only cake left on the tray was the initial slice I had cut.

I felt so discouraged and full and bloated that I decided not to go to the gym that day or the next. On the third day, I got a call from one of my gym buddies.

"Why weren't you at the gym for the last two days?" he asked.

"I'll be there this afternoon," I told him, finally putting away my guilt.

I did go that day, and the day after that, and the one after that too. Rain or shine, because my gym mates have been there to encourage me, I have not missed a day of training since then, and I've been pretty good with my diet too. We keep each other in check.

This is how it is when it comes to prayer and the spiritual walk. We start off motivated but fall once, twice, and then get discouraged and think that it's not worth the effort. If you want to persevere you will need to surround yourself with others who are on the same mission as you—to know, love, and serve Jesus.

You are a social being, and you will find God not only in your personal relationship with him but also as you give and receive God's love from others.

I am so very grateful for community in all ways. My first faith community was my family, then my first youth group, and then the Marana Thà community. All of these communities pointed me to Jesus and helped me recognize his love for me and his purpose for my life. They reached out to me and were patient, even though they may have had many reasons to give up on me. They taught me to use my gifts and talents to build others up and to live not for my own needs but to give hope and respite to others. Community is essential to our spiritual growth. It was certainly essential to mine.

As I went through a period of intense change, the power of prayer and the togetherness of community revived me. Like a fresh ocean breeze, my way of thinking and acting became clear. I realized that if I held fast to three ideals when I prayed, I could keep myself grounded and God would give me just what I needed. You can apply these to your life to gain a firmer foundation in your growth with God.

1. VISION. Where do you want to be and what do you want to achieve? Sometimes the vision is vague, like, "I know I want to serve God and the community" or "I know I want to get out of this pattern of behavior." At other times it is a clearer, more long-term picture. Set your goals and remind yourself daily of what you want to achieve. What are you praying for? What are you believing for? What is your vision, and what are your goals? Write them down, pin them up, and remind yourself of them daily.

2. PERSISTENCE. Keep asking, keep seeking, and keep knocking at God's door. Motivation may be what gets you started, but you need the discipline to keep going. Make a commitment to daily prayer and staying with the community. Commit to getting closer to the sacraments, and find the support and discipline to stick with it. If you want to see more references in the Bible about prayer, see

- 1 Thessalonians 5:17
- Ephesians 6:18
- Acts 1:14
- John 17:1
- Luke 11:1
- Psalm 39:12

You will see the fruit of your prayer if you are persistent. I am always encouraged by St. Monica, who prayed for the conversion of her son for thirty years. Her son became the greatest saint of all—St. Augustine. Hold on and don't let go!

3. ACCOUNTABILITY. Surround yourself with people who can support and intercede with you. There is power in praying with others. Jesus himself told his disciples that "if two of you on earth agree about anything they ask for, it will be done for them by my Father in heaven" (Mt 18:19). Reach out to others to support you. Connect with people who can encourage you to pray every day. You can get involved in a parish prayer group or try to meet up with some friends or family members and pray together. If you don't have people to meet with, you might be able to reach out to people to pray with you and keep you accountable through social media, e-mail, or a good, old-fashioned telephone call.

Sometimes following God's will means making decisions other people might not understand. It wasn't until after I was in seminary that my dad supported my calling to be a priest.

THREE

Run to Jesus

Summer turned to winter, the tourists disappeared, and Malta lay peacefully at rest for the quiet months. The bougainvillea was replaced by fields of gold as a carpet of glorious cape sorrel returned with the cooler days.

I was experiencing the love of God in a profound way. My desire to pray and spend time with Jesus was insatiable. I could not think and talk about God enough. I had discovered a great treasure and wanted the whole world to know about it. I would spend hours praying, reading the Bible, and thinking of ways I could let the world experience the peace and love I was experiencing. I knew that I wanted to serve God for all of my life.

The problem was that I already had a plan for my life.

At the time, I was reading for a degree in commerce at the University of Malta. With my acquired management, marketing, and economics knowledge, I was going to take over my father's home furnishing business. In my free time, I was going to travel around the world preaching and singing about Jesus. I was also going to get married and have kids.

My plan was being fulfilled so far. I was doing well at university, and during my study breaks I would travel with Dr. John, leading worship, preaching, and talking about Jesus. I also had a serious but on-and-off girlfriend, someone I'd met in the youth group. I hadn't quite got to the part where I was considering a commitment to the seminary just yet, so we were just enjoying our time together.

Life was exciting, fulfilling, and somewhat predictable, and I loved that.

One day I went, as I did every month, to receive the Sacrament of Reconciliation. I walked into a parish church I had not been to before and into the confessional. During our conversation, the priest asked me if I'd ever considered becoming a priest.

"Why do you say that, Father?" I asked, surprised by his query.

"No particular reason, I just thought you would make a good priest."

I could not get out of the confessional quick enough. A priest? Again? Why me? I did not want to become a priest. I wanted to serve God but not at the expense of a family or my freedom!

I didn't flee the building, like I would have in the past, but I knelt in that church and prayed: "God, I want to serve you more than anything else. I will sing, preach, and I'll even dance for you, but please, Jesus, *please*, do not call me to be a priest."

I was convinced that the priesthood would require too much from me, more than I could ever give. The priests I knew were lovely people, but they didn't seem to have the joy and freedom I so wanted to share with the world. They were old men in their black shirts and white collars who never smiled and spent their entire lives in a church (or so I thought). Priesthood seemed so cut off from my reality. Plus, I could not deal with the idea of celibacy and not having a wife and children to share my life with.

I did not sleep that night, plagued with doubts and worries, but I soon got over it. I forgot the words of the priest, and I completed my university degree. I spent the following months travelling around Europe, leading people in worship through music, and supporting Dr. John in his ministry.

Life was on track!

≈

One morning during prayers—this was when I was with Dr. John on one of our trips—I heard the call again. I spent time speaking to the Holy Spirit, meditating on the Word, and journaling what I heard him speak in the depth of my heart.

I wrote the words I heard that morning: "Rob, you will one day lead many people in the greatest form of worship."

I thought it meant that the music ministry I had been dreaming about would grow into something really special and I would lead worship in big arenas across the world. This gave me a great sense of peace. God's vision for me was lining up with my own vision! In fact, I got quite excited about this prospect and ran to Dr. John to tell him about what I heard.

Dr. John had a different opinion.

"I think that God is calling you to the priesthood, to celebrate the highest worship: the Mass for his people," he said.

My heart sank because I had plans, and becoming a priest was definitely not part of those plans.

Our hope is in you alone
Strong tower and endless grace

from the song
"No Greater Love"

But Dr. John wasn't done. He placed a hand on my shoulder and said in his gentle voice, "Go back to your room, and speak to God about that."

I did. I wrestled with God that day. I wanted to serve God but not through the priesthood.

I needed to see things clearly. I needed God to show me the way. "God, you know I do not want to be a priest, but if it is your will, please give me the desire for it."

I am so grateful for Dr. John. He was the one who taught me to recognize the voice of God. I felt like young Samuel who heard God call his name but did not recognise God's voice. He ran to Eli's room thinking that it was Eli who called. Eli eventually helped Samuel recognise God's voice that day thousands of years ago (see 1 Samuel 3). I felt exactly the same way with Dr. John.

We all need an Eli in our lives—people who have been on the faith journey longer than we have. We need someone we can reach out to who can help us recognize when God is speaking to us, a person who can help us listen and respond to his voice. A spiritual director. Fr. Joe had served that role for quite some time, and now Dr. John was there too.

I didn't get my answer that day, but I learned the value of my Eli.

≋

It was the summer of 2002, and Dr. John's ministry took us to Acireale, a coastal city in Catania on the eastern seaboard of Sicily, right at the foot of the famous Mount Etna. We stayed at the La Perla Ionica, a large hotel that sits by the ocean, overlooking the Ionian Sea. I remember the hotel clearly, but not for the reasons you might think—my grandfather had died some years earlier of a heart attack in one of the hotel rooms while on holiday.

We were picked up from the hotel and taken to the venue where the service was to take place. As the first song began, I noticed a charismatic young priest walk in with a group of teenagers. They participated enthusiastically in the singing and later took to the stage to teach us one of their own songs. They created such a wonderful atmosphere and I was so impressed by the priest and his young people. They cared, they were committed, and more importantly, they were young! They were closer to my age than others at the service, which I thought was fantastic. Even back then, I was drawn towards other young people in the church.

The priest's name was Giovanni Saccà. Padre Giovanni, as he was known, was in his late twenties and rarely without a smile. He looked so happy and comfortable in his vocation to the priesthood. I could not take my eyes off him and his young people throughout the service. I was drawn in by their joy and love for the Lord. I was even more taken by how young Padre Giovanni was. I couldn't even believe he was a priest!

He was, without a doubt, the coolest, hippest priest I have ever seen.

Padre Giovanni had a lot of time for me. He listened to me and answered my many questions about the priesthood. He let me tag along as he visited his parishioners and as he prayed for others. Padre Giovanni had a particular skill for leading souls who felt tormented to the healing hands of God. I loved watching him pray and give hope to so many people who came to him for direction and prayers of deliverance. My faith grew immensely watching him live out his priesthood with such great joy. I wanted to be just like him.

After the service, I had a long conversation with Padre Giovanni and the young people in his group, questioning them on why and how they were so passionate about Jesus.

I had a million questions because I had never seen a priest so in love with Jesus, for the people he served, and so comfortable in his own skin. I asked him about the priesthood and why he chose to become a priest. I asked what it was like to give up so much. I wanted to know how he worked with young people. I admired him greatly, and suddenly, I saw my future change.

I went home that night and prayed, "Lord, if I can be anything like this man, I will consider the priesthood."

I was so taken with Padre Giovanni that I invited him and his young people to come to Malta later in the summer to hang out with our youth group, and they accepted. From then on, Padre Giovanni and I would catch up often, and the more I saw him live out his priestly vocation, the more open my heart was to the priesthood.

For me, the attraction to the priesthood was not a supernatural or transcendent one. I often wondered if this is why I resisted the call so fervently—I was so aware of my humanity and my failings, and I thought that priests had to be a model of perfection. I always believed that priests had a higher calling. As those who helped connect the community to God, they had to be beyond reproach and loyal only to their "first love": God. I later grew in my understanding that the ministerial priesthood is not about the perfection of the priest but about God working in and through the priest in spite of his human weakness. Seeing this amazing mercy play throughout his life, he then has a greater responsibility to respond to the call of holiness.

Padre Giovanni was all those things, but I was drawn by the humanity and simplicity that he offered his congregation. He was practical. He worked with young people, he loved Jesus, and I felt his impact in a thousand ways. He quickly became my role model and another inspirational mentor.

≋

The call to join the priesthood was growing stronger with Padre Giovanni in my life, but I still wasn't quite ready to take the plunge, not yet. I had so many questions, so many doubts and obstacles. For one thing, I was still dating the girl from the youth group.

I decided that the time had come to talk to my girlfriend about my dilemma. I wasn't sure how she would take it, but the truth was, the discussion could no longer be ignored. Thoughts of the priesthood were coming up daily.

We spoke and decided to end the relationship. I shake my head thinking about it, as if the value of our relationship ending can be boiled down to a single sentence. Even though it was one of the hardest decisions I had ever made, I knew that I could not properly discern my possible vocation to the priesthood while still in a committed relationship. To even contemplate joining the priesthood meant that I needed to experience communion between myself and God alone. That was the only way I believed that I could listen to what God was telling me.

Many tears were shed as we dissolved our relationship, but to this day, we are still good friends. She is now happily married and has a wonderful family.

Just so you know, making the decision to live a celibate life was not an easy one. People often ask me how I can survive without sex. I suppose it's like anyone else. Even in a married relationship, one of true love and respect, there is a need for self-control and restraint. We have the power to control our urges, especially when we love and respect the one whom we love. My decision to be celibate was one I made and live out with great joy; however, the reality is that my mind knows I'm celibate but my body has no idea.

This is why I need to keep my heart focused on my first love: Jesus. I pray and meditate every day; I exercise and direct my creative energy into music and building up the lives of others. At times, I do wonder what it would be like to have my own family, but I also find great peace in my call to live for others in this way.

Commitment is a strange thing. When we commit to anything we are choosing to say no to a thousand other options. But if we commit to something out of love there will be more freedom in that one commitment than a thousand options. When a young man or woman chooses to get married, they are saying yes to their bride or groom and no to their other options. They do not need to say yes to their spouse and no to the other options only once but every day for the rest of their lives. It is the same with the celibate priesthood. Every day I have to choose Jesus and live for him alone, and this is not possible if I do not have an ongoing relationship with him.

Breaking up with my girlfriend removed the first obstacle to that relationship.

The second obstacle was that in order to study for the priesthood, I had to give up my independence and move into the seminary for seven years. Seven years! Can you imagine that? Having already completed a degree, I would need to spend a further seven years studying hard to become a priest. I was going to have to surrender my music, my dreams of travel, and my plan of having a family.

A third and even greater obstacle was telling my parents. My dad had built the home furnishing business with the expectation that I would take over when he retired. He had his own dreams for my success and happiness, and the priesthood did not figure in them one little bit. I would have to shatter every idea he ever had of me and break his heart.

≋

In October 2003, after many months of going to daily Mass, praying for guidance, and fulfilling a commitment to an hour of Eucharistic Adoration three times a week, I was close to making my decision.

Dr. John had been helping me through this time, but he wasn't the only one. I had a chat with Padre Giovanni in which we talked about what I could expect in the seminary. I admired him so much, but I wanted to know how he coped with celibacy and if he got lonely. Did he ever regret becoming a priest? What about the seminary? Would I be able to survive that for seven or eight years?

He gave me that joyful laugh of his, and smiled at me patiently. "Stop torturing yourself and make a decision, Rob," he said. "The most important thing I can tell you is that my time in the seminary deepened my connection with Jesus."

For me, that was it. That was what I needed to hear. My love for Jesus was all-consuming. It was all that mattered to me. The things I'd seen as obstacles were shifted to one side. I decided to pick up the phone and make an appointment with the rector of the seminary known as the Archbishop's Seminary in Rabat, Malta.

The moment had come.

After years of wrestling with it, I was ready to answer what I believed to be God's call.

I met up with the rector and arranged to spend a few days in the seminary just watching and observing. I was nervous on my first morning, but it didn't take long for my anxiety to disappear. I was surprised at how normal everything was. The seminary was filled with men who were all just ordinary human beings seeking to know and serve God.

I made my formal application to join the seminary.

After a few weeks of nervous waiting, I received the news that the rector and the Archbishop of Malta accepted me into the seminary. My intake was just a few weeks away in December.

When I found out, I was filled with great joy and a deep sense of peace. Everything felt right. All the fears and obstacles I had were overshadowed by the prospect of serving God through the priesthood.

≈

The whole experience of "will I/won't I" was a little like skydiving. If you are scared of heights like I am, the mere thought of jumping out of a plane at 12,500 feet in the air would freak you out. You go through the debrief, you put on your flight suit and parachute, and then you wait. By the time you get to the plane, you're trembling with fear. As the plane takes off, your anxiety heightens, and before jumping out of the plane, you seemingly go in and out of consciousness.

"One! Two! *Jump!*" shouts the instructor.

You muster up the courage to jump, and once you do, you forget all the fear, all the anxiety, and experience nothing but pure freedom and exhilaration.

So many men and women have heard God's call over their lives but are simply afraid to jump. They hold on to the side of the plane so they can keep their options open, but the reality, as mentioned earlier, is that you will find more freedom in one commitment than in having a thousand options. There is nothing more beautiful and fulfilling than responding to the call of God. I love being a priest, and if I had a thousand lifetimes where I was called a thousand times, I would choose to say yes to the priesthood in each one.

I am not saying that saying yes to God is easy. It doesn't offer a lifetime of bliss—quite the contrary. Seeking and following God's will is tough and requires a constant death to self. I'm not sure if you know those words. It's not really a common phrase, but it's at the core of how I see myself as a Christian and a priest.

Death to self is an act of ongoing surrender, an ongoing decision to choose the love of others over a love for ourselves. *Death to self* is choosing to serve others because it builds them up. As a priest, I choose to live for God and my community because we have faith that we're building an eternal, rather than a temporal, kingdom. My purpose in life is to help others build a relationship with Jesus Christ, and to do that, I must serve their needs.

While I still acknowledge myself and my physical needs, I try to be heaven-minded and motivated by a love for others and for God. I try to put charity and care at the forefront of everything, not my own wants.

I think it's a good lesson whether you have a calling to the priesthood or not. The world would be a much kinder place if we put the needs of others first. Our prime example? Jesus came to show us this by the way in which he lived and died.

Death to self can be likened to a parent with their child. They give up everything for the child, often making personal sacrifices such as working jobs they don't necessarily enjoy, making sure the child is fed before they feed themselves, and sometimes putting their personal safety at risk to ensure the child is safe and protected. When experiencing death to self for their child, they are doing it out of absolute love and with faith that the child will grow up strong and happy because of their actions. That is their motivation. That is their fulfillment.

When it comes to living for God and others, we need that same love and faith. For God and for others. True and authentic death to self is not possible without love and faith. It is a practice which requires discipline, one which we have to grow within us. It takes small acts of kindness and selflessness every day to build a death to self attitude, and though I am far from perfecting this, it is this that motivates me to work hard in my parish and my ministry.

Responding to God's call requires you to take up your own cross and, often, the cross of the multitudes. The good news is that abundant grace and strength comes with every obstacle you face.

Jesus said, "Take up [your] cross and follow me" (Mt 16:24). It is not easy to live for God and for others. Our natural inclination is to live for ourselves and to work for our own success and survival. But the reality is we are human beings dependent on a God who can help us reach our potential, and we need a community that will help us to reach the transcendent. In order to reach out to others and to God, we need to deny ourselves, to acknowledge a death to self. Jesus also says there is no greater love than to lay down one's life (see John 15:13).

Even now, when I am feeling depressed and immersed in my own selfish woes, I will pray, "God, please send someone who is worse off than me so that I will not worry about my own self, but have the privilege to care for them."

My fears about joining the priesthood were washed away the moment I jumped. I haven't lost my freedom and I find serving God exhilarating. All I had to do was commit.

Once I got accepted into the seminary, I still had a few issues to sort out. The obstacles I encountered might have been pushed to the side as I committed to God, but I knew at some point I'd need to come back to them. Telling my parents was one of those obstacles. What would they think? I was filled with anxiety.

I knew it would be easier starting with Mum, so I sat down at the kitchen table while she was preparing lunch. I can still remember the sound of the knife hitting the chopping board; the air was filled with the fresh scent of eggplant and capsicum, the sizzle of oil and garlic from the frying pan, and the floury smell of breadcrumbs.

I swallowed my nerves and ignored my hunger. It was now or never. "Mum, I am going to become a priest."

She glanced up from the chopping board, and for a moment, I saw her fight a need to leap for joy. She was overcome with emotion, but to keep her cool she looked back at the food she was cooking. Then the knife suddenly went still, she took a deep breath, and with her eyes tearing up, she said, "I'm so glad you finally realized it."

She knew! Of course, she knew.

Mum knew I was going to become a priest long before I ever did. She reminded me of that vision she had years earlier. I had completely forgotten about it, but my mother had held that vision close to her heart, praying that it would come true. She could not have been happier and prouder of me, and as she came around to where I was sitting and wrapped me in her arms, everything just felt so right.

After that, I told my friends and other relatives. Many responded with surprise, but others, including my old friend Daniel, saw it coming. My great-aunt, a cloistered nun living in Valletta whom I'd only met a few times before, had been praying for years that a member of our family would be called to the priesthood. I had not known.

When I walked into the monastery to ask her to pray for me as I began my discernment, my period to recognise my vocation to the priesthood, she responded in her gentle voice, "So you're the one!"

She knew that God would answer her prayer, and once again I got to witness years of labor, the work of prayer, being answered.

I tried to hold off telling my father for as long as I could, but as I had discovered when fighting my addictions, you cannot outrun everything. Sooner or later, word was going to reach him, and it was best that it came from me. The time had come to break the news.

I knew he wouldn't be happy. He had spent his whole life building his business—starting as a sixteen-year-old in a corner store selling mattresses, pillows, inflatable beach mats, toy buckets, and spades—to become one of Malta's largest and most successful home furnishing companies. As much as I had plans, so did he. He had always planned that his eldest son would follow his path and work in the family business. That was me.

I hated the idea of disappointing him, and I was nervous about breaking my news. This announcement required more strategic planning than my conversation with Mum. Dad was coming home for lunch, so what I did was choose the spot where he always ate as my ambush zone. I prepared the dining room for a quick escape, just in case he got too upset about what I was about to tell him. I opened two doors, one on either side of the dining room, and then I waited for him to sit down with his food. I walked through one door, paused for a moment, gathered my wits and said, "Daddy, I am going to become a priest."

No response.

He sat there and continued eating like I hadn't even spoken.

I was strung pretty tight and ready to spring through the door. I knew he would answer me eventually; I just had to wait.

He looked up at me with his stately gaze and said, "If that's what you want to do, then do it."

I was surprised by his answer, but I knew there was more to it than that. I was sure that he was hiding his true feelings. I left the dining room quietly, leaving him to his lunch. At some point, I knew I'd get a clearer idea of what was going through his mind.

His employees later told me that he spent the next day in absolute silence. Someone later saw him leaning against a wall, crying. He was sad, disappointed, and upset, and he thought that I was disillusioned and wasting my entire life on what he thought was a passing phase of religious fanaticism. He was anxious about what he would tell his friends and felt that, in some way, my choice was an indication of his failure as a parent.

I didn't think that way at all; he was never a failure in my eyes, but for a short time, our communication was virtually nonexistent.

A few weeks later, I reached out to my father for help as I needed to buy a few things prior to entering the seminary. Among the things I needed was a *cassock*, a black garment worn by seminarians during prayer and liturgies. I asked him for the money to buy this vestment and he refused to help me, suggesting that I get it off a priest who has left the priesthood.

I could see then that he was afraid. He was scared that I was making a rash decision and would not be happy, successful, and fulfilled as a priest. It's a fear that many parents have for their children, and it derives from love. With the support of Mum, communication was nearly back to normal as December approached and my intake drew nigh, but

I could still sense his underlying tension. However, I'm sure he saw my commitment to this new path.

Dad might have shown resistance to my decision, but I loved him then as I love him now. I am close to him today, and I do not think that there is anyone more proud of me than he is. For some reason, his breakthrough to acceptance came much later when I was offered a record deal towards the end of my first year in the seminary. I had started appearing on radio and television, and it was then he caught a glimpse of my happiness, joy, and success in the priesthood. It was like it all clicked for him, and there it was, I could suddenly see how proud he was of my path. But those days were still to come. Back then, we coexisted in a tense place.

I graduated from university with my business degree and entered the seminary by December, all in the one year. Now that I was leaving my home, my mother, my family, my friends, Dr. John, and the Marana Thà community, I was both excited and sad. I was excited at the thought of living in a large community of like-minded people who wanted to give their lives in service of God and of others, but I was also sad that I was leaving behind the security and love of my family home. Rachel and Joseph, Mum, and even Dad were all so supportive, and in their loving faces I was reminded of how blessed I was.

Things had progressed so quickly that December arrived in a flash. Once I was inside the seminary, I had a pleasant surprise when it turned out that I didn't need to completely cut off my old life. I was still able to visit friends and family on weekends and occasionally attend Marana Thà community gatherings. I still had my music too. Some of my fellow seminarians enjoyed hearing me practice on the guitar. I even got to write a couple of songs with some of my seminarian brothers, such as "Nothing Less," a track which you'll find on my *Closer* album.

I also helped care for my friend Daniel. He was quickly succumbing to his disease, as those with severe muscular dystrophy do. We had been close friends for so many years, and I believe that I learned a lot about compassion and caring for others from my relationship with him. I feel that this experience really benefited my studies and helped me understand the true meaning of death to self. It helped me understand what service to the community meant, too. And importantly, I got to spend time with my dear friend.

I still harbored a couple of fears as I entered the seminary. I was committed in my decision, that was no issue, but I still feared that I would have to give up the dream of my wider music ministry, travel, and family on a permanent basis. In my heart, I still really wanted to have kids and my own family. Despite all of my prayers and conversations with people like Dr. John and Padre Giovanni, I hadn't been able to completely erase that desire. I had even wondered if it would lead to me dropping out of the seminary before I was ordained.

The other thing on my mind, and it was a far more pressing issue as I walked through those doors in December, was that I would be locked up in the seminary for years with people who I didn't quite understand. That probably sounds strange coming from a priest, but if you look at the process I went through, I had only recently come around to my decision to discern the priesthood. A lot of the seminarians knew they would become priests from when they were children. I hadn't considered the priesthood until a year prior. They knew all the right jargon and rituals and had a lot of time to think about it as they grew up. They would also have spent a lot of time talking about it.

This was a massive culture shock for me. I had strong faith and I wanted the community of seminarians, but I didn't quite know much about the practice and ritual in a formal way. My relationship with God was very sponta- neous and was born in a different environment to the other seminarians. I had a lot to learn about liturgy and ritual.

I loved that I was surrounded by men who wanted to serve God with their entire lives, but many of them expressed their love and devotion in a very different way than I did. Some had a very structured way of addressing God, whereas others were very silent and meditative. I, on the other hand, only knew how to address God spon- taneously and from my heart. I later learned to appreciate the riches of structured prayers and devotions and studied hard to fold them into my worship, but right at the start I felt all at sea.

In time, I grew to love my new community. We lived, prayed, studied, and relaxed together. We had good times and times when arguments got very heated. We were like rough rocks beneath the waves, chipping against each other until they become smooth pebbles.

Even the way they thought about God was different from mine. I remember the first argument I ever had at the seminary. It was with one of my first year companions. We were sitting at a table talking about whether we should expect things from God or not. He thought that things should be prayed for and that it was presumptuous to expect things from God, but I thought differently. "It's not that we deserve it," I explained to him, "but God wants us to have expectations because he loves us. Just like when I go home, I expect my bed to still be there and food to be in the fridge. I don't deserve my bed to be there. I did nothing to earn or deserve my bed at home with my parents. But I'm sure it would be quite offensive to my parents if one day I decided not to go home because I didn't expect there to be a bed and a welcome at home."

This heated argument ended with a pencil thrown at my head.

But it wasn't all arguments and pencil warfare.

We would often play practical jokes on each other. We were, after all, young men! I remember one time, one of the seminarians went to use the bathroom at the end of the hallway. When he was in the bathroom, a group of us completely emptied his bedroom of absolutely everything. I can't remember if it was inspired by our earlier argument, but it seemed like a good idea at the time.

We never had much in our rooms, but we had to move quickly, regardless. He came back to his room to find his bed, his cupboard, and all his other belongings had disappeared. We'd hidden them in the room next door and a few of us were breathless from our efforts, but it was worth it to see the look of confusion on his face.

We would often have water fights too; after all, Malta can get quite hot and cassocks don't really breathe too well. Outside or inside, it didn't really matter—where there was water there was trouble. When an innocent seminarian took the time to wash his floor, if someone was nearby and looking to cause some mischief, he would take the dirty water and throw it back over the clean floor.

Everything was done with a light heart, and often, the mischief-maker would help with any cleaning up.

It was always reassuring to me that we could laugh and joke, and very quickly, my fears about the strictures of seminary life disappeared.

From the feedback I've had over the years, I think people might believe that seminary is just a group of serious men doing serious things all the time. It's so much more than

that, but mostly it's just normal, ordinary people learning
how best they can serve God.

≈

One of the harder parts of living in the seminary is that not
all people who enter stay until the end. It's worth noting
that this is not the point of the seminary. It's not a fully
structured seven-year degree program. The seminary allows
young men to spend months, *years*, reflecting on whether
this call is for them. It's about discernment.

There are those who decide to leave. I can only specu-
late on the personal reasons why. Some may have felt that
it would cost them more than they could afford, humanly
or even spiritually speaking, or that they would be better
off serving their community in a different way. There were
those who chose a path like Dr. John with his community
faith group and those who revelled in their daily worship
but wanted a family too. I understood the challenge. I had
faced those same concerns.

The first time one of my brother seminarians announced
that he was leaving, I was shocked. I cried for days at the loss
of his company. You build such close friendships with the
other seminarians that losing them is like losing a brother.
This eventually became less of a surprise, less of a hurt, and
I began to realize that this is the point of the seminary and
of discernment.

Just because you enter the seminary doesn't mean that
you are called to be a priest. The time we spend studying
and learning and living is a process of discerning whether
this is the life for you or not. It takes a lot of courage to leave
if you realize that the priesthood is not for you.

I admire those men, the ones who listen to what's within
and choose to go. They all had the courage to recognize that
being a priest was not for them and to follow their hearts. It

takes willpower to stay on the path of seminary formation when you do realize that it may not be for you. You fight against yourself and God's will when you push against what God is trying to tell you, when you try and do right for the wrong reasons. God has a way for all of us to serve, and it doesn't follow that it has to be the same for everyone.

The challenges were coming for me as well. The days can be long at the seminary, and a certain amount of discipline is encouraged. I had always been so spontaneous in my worship that the structured days were hard. We began our days so early. Many mornings I would try and think of excuses as to why I should not get out of bed, but I could never find any valid ones.

When I found myself making excuses, I asked myself if I wanted to leave. I wondered if I could survive a life living entirely for others and alone, without a family. Sure, I was surrounded by many priests and seminarians then, but what if I was eventually sent to a parish where there wasn't the support and accountability I had at the seminary? Would I survive without a spiritual family of my own? I did not want to become a priest only to become disillusioned and leave. I needed to discern this call well.

In truth, I was horrified at even thinking such thoughts, but as I'd seen some of my brothers leave, I had to entertain it and give it space to breathe and find voice. If I repressed those feelings, things could have been terrible. Allowing my doubts to surface allowed me to know what my heart wanted. And in doing so, the answer came to me quickly, and I never struggled with my decision after that.

You see, the decision to join was hard but not as hard as the idea of ever leaving. I knew that what sat before me was a choice between *good* and *best*, not between bad and good. I never would have thought that way even a year or so earlier, but that's how it was. I didn't have any bad options ahead of me, only good ones.

Seminary formation trains the seminarian in how to listen to the heart, how to listen to the voice of God, and how to find the strength and courage with the help of the community to press on. If a seminarian realizes that the call to priesthood is not for their life, they can walk away in peace and joy, knowing that they were listening to God when they made their decision.

≈

Discerning my vocation to the priesthood was a long process, and I didn't take it lightly. Just as I believe that God has a plan for me, God has a plan for your life too. He has an awesome plan, and if you can figure it out and have the courage to step into it, you will live a life more fulfilled than you could ever imagine.

"'For I know the plans I have for you,' declares the LORD, 'plans to prosper you and not to harm you, plans to give you hope and a future'" (Jer 29:11).

There is nothing more fulfilling than knowing that you are doing what your creator created you to be and do. To discover the will of God for your life does not necessarily ask you to commit to the priesthood or religious life or to become a missionary in a far-off land but to discover how God has called you to live out your relationship and your communion with the Church. The first and most important call is to get to heaven, to be like Jesus, to be holy, to be a saint. God knows how to get you there. His will for your life is in line with that primary call.

Finding out God's will for your life can be challenging. The practice of discernment, of obtaining spiritual direction, surrounding yourself with the right people, and understanding God's Word through reflection and prayer means giving ourselves over to God and his will.

Here are a few steps I took to discerning God's will for my life, steps which you can also take to figure out what God wants for your life. Remember, when you follow God's will, you often have a choice between *good* and *best*, not good and bad.

1. **LISTEN TO THE CHURCH.** Even though I had forgotten it, my mother had given me the first hint of what God intended for my life through that vision of me as a priest years earlier. A couple of priests over the years encouraged me to consider the priesthood and so did some of my close Christian friends. People who I looked up to as mentors—Dr. John and Padre Giovanni—also suggested the same and eventually the rector of the seminary in Malta and the Archbishop did as well. Although you have to make the decision yourself, lend an ear to the believing community because God speaks through the Church.

2. **SEEK SPIRITUAL DIRECTION.** Find someone who is wiser and more advanced in their walk with Jesus. Give them permission to speak into your life, and then listen to what you believe God is saying to you. They will discern with you and help you listen to the gentle voice of God, especially when the voice of emotion (excitement, fear, anxiety, love, or hate) gets distracting. Be honest with your spiritual directors and allow them to be honest with you.

3. **LOOK FOR ROLE MODELS.** If you think that God might be calling you to something, find someone you can learn from. Once I felt that the Holy Spirit might be calling me to the priesthood, I met up with Padre Giovanni regularly. I wanted to learn and understand what the priesthood was, what priests did in their free time, how they reacted to pastoral situations, and what it was like to live a celibate life. Don't

idealize your role models, but keep your eyes open and be willing to learn from their mistakes and imperfections. If you, for some reason, can't physically and practically be around such a person or people, try to find people you can learn from online through such avenues as social media and You-Tube. I have many role models that I follow from all around the world. I learn from them on Instagram, Snapchat and Twitter.

4. **PRAY.** Speak to God; ask him what he wants from your life. Listen. Take some time to let him speak to your heart. Consider keeping a journal, and write down what you believe God is impressing on your heart. Take that journal to your spiritual director, and let them help you discern what is of God and what is not. Keep close to the sacraments—particularly the Eucharist and Reconciliation. Keeping your spirit clean and nourished will allow you to listen more attentively. When listening, you might not hear audible words, but as you surround yourself with the practices of God, you will slowly begin to put on his mindset, desiring the things that honor him and his will.

5. **CONSIDER WHAT BRINGS YOU JOY.** Although God most certainly will call you out of your comfort zone, once you take the leap of faith, joy will follow. If you walk in a relationship with Jesus, then joy is already imprinted in your heart, you just need to figure it out and embrace it. "[God's] word is very near you; it is in your mouth and in your heart so you may obey it" (Dt 30:14). I knew that I wanted to help people and to encourage people in their faith. That gave me joy. Once I was able to overcome the fear, the idea of being a priest also brought me joy.

6. **DO IT SCARED.** Once you think you might know what God intends for your life, do it. Even if you are not 100 percent certain. You will never know for sure until you take the leap. Don't wait for more confirmation; just do it! Don't wait for

the fear to go away, but do it scared. If it could possibly be God's will for your life, and it does not go against his Word and the teachings of the Church, then don't hold back!

Being a servant of God means serving God's people wherever they need you.

FOUR

At the Foot of the Cross

G oing to the seminary was like going back to school. I quickly settled into a regimen of prayer, meals, classes, and study. The morning bell would ring at 5:30 a.m., and the fifty seminarians would gather in the beautiful but cold marble chapel for an hour and a half of prayer, meditation, and Mass. It was tough to fit into the discipline of early morning prayer at first, but I soon learned to appreciate and even love offering the first waking hours of every day to the Lord with my brother seminarians. Proverbs 3:9 says, "Honor the LORD with your wealth, with the firstfruits of all your crops." A sense of peace flowed into the day as I began this now lifelong discipline of being present with God every morning.

Prayer was followed by a quick breakfast before taking the seminary bus to the department of theology and philosophy at the University of Malta—a state-run university where we would attend lectures and study for most of the day. We need to be well-qualified for our work. A priest often serves as a counsellor and spiritual adviser. We are there for people at the worst and best moments of their lives. We are trained to work in and build communities as well as build churches and help administer schools. A priest is an evangelist and a teacher of the faith, a conflict resolver, and has to know how to be a good and just employer. We administer sacraments, defend the faith, and help build people to become all that God has called them to be. We study philosophy, theology, anthropology, sociology, and psychology, as well as canon law and business administration.

Seminarians study, *a lot*. The studies we undertake are designed to help us understand how people think, how they act in society, and how they understand and reach out to God. This process of study also helps us to look within ourselves and see how we do the same. Many of us end up with two or three degrees and a Masters in theology.

I often found my studies quite stressful, as like normal students we had to deliver essays and take exams. But despite the hard work, it never failed to be interesting. It has such a bearing on our work, especially the psychology and sociology teachings, so I studied hard. As someone who values work in the community, it's vital that I have a powerful understanding of *how* people work. We provide more than just religious instruction—we are also community service workers. We *must* have the education to support our parishioners the best we can.

Aside from its practical purpose, going to university was a wonderful opportunity to break from seminary routine and hang out with young men and women from all walks of life. Some people attended the same classes as us to deepen their faith, while others wanted to prove that God was a mere invention of man—a crutch for those who cannot handle the pressures of life. Needless to say, we had some interesting debates in class!

At 4 p.m., after a long day of study and hanging out at one of the university's many cafes, we would get picked up by the bus and taken back to the seminary where we would spend a couple of hours catching up with our study assignments. After that we would gather again for evening prayer at 6 p.m., followed by dinner.

Dinner was a time to catch up with my brother seminarians, whom I grew to love and appreciate. We would often talk about our day over a meal of meat, vegetables, pasta, and hot Maltese bread, something that I would demolish with gusto.

At 9 p.m., after dinner and a bit of free time, we would go to the chapel to pray our night prayer before heading back to our rooms for the night. In my free time, I would often play my guitar and sometimes gather with my fellow seminarians to sing a few songs.

There were times when the days felt way too long, but after a while I got used to it. In fact, I grew to love studying, and the intervals of prayer throughout my day taught me to practice the presence of God, to be aware of his presence and turn to him throughout my day. The routine may have been difficult at first, but I grew to love it as it helped me get closer to God.

I still use this discipline today, turning my first thoughts of the day to God and taking moments to pray wherever I am: in my bedroom, my office, the church, a hotel room, backstage before a concert, or on a plane. I have also learned to end every day by reviewing the events of the day, thanking God for the good moments, and asking for grace to serve him better then next day.

Every day in the seminary followed the same general routine, except for Saturdays and Sunday mornings. On weekends, we were sent out to do community or pastoral work within a local parish or religious organization.

During my time in the seminary, I got to work with the disabled and elderly. I also worked on a mission to help women get out of prostitution, and for one year, I spent every Saturday serving as a chaplain in a high-security juvenile detention center.

While working with the women who trawled the cruel streets of Malta and kids in detention as young as ten years old, I began to realize that *this* was what I wanted to spend the rest of my life doing. I wanted to help the young offenders recognize their dignity and worth, even in their place of despair. These children were in the highest security juvenile prison for serious crimes such as murder, rape, and acts of terrorism. And some of the women I worked with on the street were just trying to pay their debts to attain freedom from their pimps. So many of them were in their teens and had lost all sense of self-worth.

How did they get to this point? In some cases, domestic violence and poverty played a part. In other cases, somewhere in their pasts these young people lost sight of who they really were; they made poor choices and forgot their beauty and dignity and their call to love and be loved unconditionally.

I felt a driving need within me to do something, and it was about this time that I knew that I was going to live for this cause—to help young people everywhere realize their dignity and worth.

Sunday afternoon was our rest time, something that I came to cherish. I would use my free afternoon to rest and think up ideas of how I could support teens. I used these days to design my website and update my Facebook and Myspace pages. Yes, I had a Myspace page. Google it—it was a thing! I'd also write songs and make lists of things I wanted to do. Travel the world with my music ministry, preach in schools, open a recording studio, create music videos . . . I often gave over my Sunday to dreaming about the future and just listening to what was inside me.

This routine brought about a rhythm which was conducive to the ongoing discernment of God's will for my life. I found the community work particularly inspiring. Working with people in their homes, in detention, and on the street showed me a new level of the expectations that God had for me. Away from so many distractions in my life, I was able to relearn simplicity—to focus on prayer and how to invest my heart and soul in the community.

You know, it's amazing how much noise there is in our lives. Most of the time we don't even realize it. There are so many things to do, people to please, pressures to live up to and commitments to keep. Seminary life was an opportunity for me to settle into a routine of simplicity and focus on letting God love and guide me.

The thing is that God speaks. He leads, corrects, and offers us consolation, but too often we don't hear him because we are too busy with our own lives to listen.

≈

One of my favorite chapters in the Bible is Psalm 46. Verse 10 says, "Be still, and know that I am God." This verse, written in Maltese, was painted above the tabernacle in the seminary chapel next to my room. *"Iskot! Kunu afu li jien Alla."* It encourages those who enter to do so in silence.

This means a lot more to the Maltese reader than anyone reading it in English. The Old Testament, including the book of Psalms, was written in Hebrew, a Semitic language. Maltese is also a Semitic language. The word *iskot,* or "be still," literally means "shut up."

I could be caught in middle of life's distractions, but every time I walked into the chapel I was reminded by God to shut up and let him take control. I was asked to lay down my distractions and stop my constant effort to do and be what people expect of me. Seminary life, in essence, taught me to shut up and let God love me, speak to me, guide me, and make me holy.

This is a lesson I still hold on to. I face constant pressure (most of it put on my shoulders by myself) to perform, to be holy, to say the right things, and to be all things to all people. My seminary formation has been instrumental in helping me recognize the need to shut up and let God give me a hug, to know that he does not want my work but my heart. He does not seek my success but my faithfulness.

As I mentioned earlier, I currently serve a parish community in rural Australia and work as the founder-director of Stronger Youth (our diocesan youth ministry). I spend much of my year on the road preaching a kerygmatic message to the multitudes.

Preaching a kerygmatic message since I left the seminary has been rewarding. *Kerygma* is the preaching or proclamation of the basic Christian Gospel. Upon this is *catechesis* (verbal instruction of doctrine). I work with a generation of young people that has never really heard the Gospel in a way that they could relate to and apply to their lives.

A lot of schools and institutions that I visit seek to catechize, to instruct people in their faith. In Malta, catechism was already very prominent because people have the basics of faith. They know the basic Christian message, which they get by attending church and by what is passed down in their family from one generation to the next.

I have found that many of the young people I work with in Australia do not know the basics of the faith: who Jesus is, why he came into this world, what he did, and why he did it. This generation hears stories of Jesus in their schoolbooks and on television but have never considered him as a real historical figure, risen from the dead and alive today, who can impact and influence their present.

I once visited a class in a Catholic high school and asked if anyone could tell me anything about Jesus the person. Some were telling me stories they had been told about him from the Bible. One student said he was like Hercules, a mythological figure who serves as an inspiration to many, especially children. Another student in the class assumed that he was not a historical figure but one out of a storybook.

This is certainly not the case in every secondary school I have visited, but it certainly is not endemic to that one school. This is why the kerygmatic message is important.

I am an evangelist at heart.

I often find myself preaching the basic Christian kerygmatic message to those who have not heard it before or to those who are disengaged. I speak of Jesus as a person I know personally, one with whom I am in love. The people I speak to are often confused or fascinated by this and want to know more. That is where I currently spend most of my time and energy. Catechesis, the instruction of doctrine, is essential to this understanding, especially if these listeners are going to continue their journey with Jesus. They cannot survive the Christian path without good instruction.

I spend a lot of time giving instruction and encouragement to the congregation in my parish and to our youth leaders, but there are only a few of us in my area going to the outskirts of our diocese and preaching the Gospel, the basic Christian message, to those who are disengaged from the Church for whatever reason. I preach using all of my tools and skills as a priest. I go to schools and play my music. I use my social media presence in a constructive way. I engage in dialogue with teenagers in any environment I can find them in, such as youth conferences, clubs, pubs, social media, YouTube, radio waves, or anywhere else that they're willing and ready to listen.

From what I've seen, young people aren't coming to church, so I live my life trying to bring the Church to them. It's a simple approach that comes from a disciplined working routine instilled in my heart from my time in the seminary and my first foray into community work on weekends.

≈

Making the decision to enter the seminary was a hard one, as you've seen. I did not know how I would cope being cut off from the world I knew for seven whole years. Ironically, I found great freedom within those seminary walls. I experienced a deep sense of consolation in the knowledge that I was somehow in the right place, fulfilling God's plan for my life. This is not to say that I knew beyond any doubt that God was calling me to the priesthood. I had my moments.

I get asked countless times how I really *knew* that God was calling me to the priesthood. Only yesterday, I received a Facebook message from a young man in South Africa asking me to pray for him as he felt called to the priesthood but would not act on it until he knew for sure that God was calling him. The reality is that you will never know for sure. Love is always a risk. What you need is a generous heart and the grace to fulfill the call will follow.

This does not only apply to the call to priesthood but also to any other vocation.

When I got the impression that God might be calling me to the priesthood, I pursued it. I took a chance. I did not, and still do not, know for sure if it was God calling me. A strange admission, I'm sure, but the thing is, if it *was* God calling me, I did not want to miss his call. Once I said yes and acknowledged that my journey would not be easy, I found that through prayer and *trying* to keep faithful to the vocation, I have abundant grace to live out what is my vocation with joy.

God does not often speak in a loud voice but gently whispers his will for our lives. I love the story of Elijah in 1 Kings 19. God leads Elijah to a mountain, away from the distractions of the world. There, Elijah hears a sound of a great wind, feels a mighty earthquake, and sees a fire. The Lord was not in any of these. Then he hears a gentle whisper. "When Elijah heard it, he pulled his cloak over his face and went out and stood at the mouth of the cave" (1 Kgs 19:13).

God whispers, and then it is up to us to respond. We can choose to listen and respond or to turn away. God will not love us any less if we do, and in his love and mercy, he will help us find joy in an alternate life path. It's kind of like the GPS in your car. The best route is calculated by the machine, but we can choose to disobey it. It pauses for a moment and then gives us an alternate route.

I imagine that if I had chosen to ignore God's call to the priesthood, he would still have blessed me in business and with a wonderful family, but I did not want to miss out on what I somehow sensed to be God's best route for my life. In other words, I could have been a great architect or an excellent businessman, but I am just not satisfied with great and excellent. Deep in my heart, even though I was scared, I sensed that God had an *awesome* plan for my life, and I wanted to pursue that.

The seminary was the place to start this awesome plan, and I had a deep sense of peace living there, but it was not easy. Routine is great, but it can sometimes get a bit dry. I missed my family and friends, and I often got tired of facing the same people and having the same topical conversations, day in and day out. There was a lot of altar talk, which I was not at all interested in. Like everyone else, seminarians can get caught up in small talk, or water-cooler talk, with conversations discussing how priests should dress and how the altar should be set up.

In our free time, I was often brought into conversations about correct and incorrect liturgical music styles and on liturgical controversies, like whether lay people should hold hands during the Lord's Prayer at Mass and whether or not there should be a sign of peace during the Mass at all.

These may or may not be valid points, but I wanted to talk about bigger, more pressing things like influencing and evangelizing young people. I wanted to talk about reaching out to a broken world, but most of the time I just wanted to have normal, non-religious conversations. I almost felt like there was an urgency and no time to waste on seemingly trivial things. This is not to say that we shouldn't give the liturgy the best we can give, but I just could not understand how some of these other young men did not seem to share the same thirst for broken souls that I did.

As time went by, I learned to join in some conversations and avoid others. At other times, I realized I had much to learn about biting my tongue and lovingly walking away. I still do.

Malta is one of the most religious countries in the world, and though I had grown up surrounded by the Catholic religion, I hadn't paid close attention to it. It soon became clear in those early days at the seminary that there was a lot about the Church I didn't know, including about the liturgy, devotions, and sacraments. I was preparing to become a priest, but I didn't know how to pray the Rosary and had never even heard about the Divine Mercy Chaplet (which is the devotion to Divine Mercy).

I had also never served as an altar server, so I was very embarrassed the first time I was asked to serve at a Mass halfway through my first year in the seminary. It was too far into the year to tell the seminary staff that I had no clue how to serve at the altar.

It was a disaster!

The seminarians looked on in embarrassment as I showed up in the wrong shoes, rang the bell at the wrong time, and accidentally blew out the candle during the Gospel reading. By the end of the Mass my nerves were shot and automation had taken over. I held the book out for the priest to read the final prayer. He looked at me, smiled, and then gently turned the book the right side up. I wanted the ground to swallow me.

Over the following years, I tried to devote myself to school, prayer, and becoming a better Catholic, including learning to know and love Jesus through the gift which is his Church. The more I learned, the more I realized that I didn't know everything, and yet the more I prayed, the deeper the longing became to share the hope I had in Jesus (see 1 Peter 3:15). I wanted to go out and tell the world about Jesus, but I did not know where to begin. I had to focus on my formation and wait patiently for my chance to serve in the world.

Weeks became months and months became years. And as they do, the years flew by.

For the sake of his sorrowful
passion, have mercy on us

from the song
"Divine Mercy Chaplet"

≋

I want to share with you a story that solidified my path, something that happened as I was about to begin my third year in the seminary. I was getting used to living the life of a seminarian, and as third-year seminarians, for the first time in our stay, we got to choose our own rooms. On the first day of term, I made my way up to the top floor of the seminary building to choose my room.

I knew straight away which room I wanted. It was the one closest to the green chapel—a small, unsightly chapel on the third floor used by senior seminarians. The small bedroom had the nicest view of the beautiful Tal Virtù valley—a stunning vista overlooking the busy fields that sweep towards the south coast of Malta—and I could conveniently go to the chapel at any time of the day or night without needing to suffer the cold of the tiled hallways.

I would spend many hours in that little chapel; praying, studying, reading, meditating, and even sleeping before Jesus in the Blessed Sacrament. Every morning, before anyone was out of their rooms, I would wake up and head straight to the chapel. I'd walk up to the front of the chapel and gently knock on the wooden tabernacle door. I would whisper, "Jesus, I'm here," and then just rest my head on the tabernacle for a few moments, imagining myself on the hill at Calvary, taking some of the weight off Jesus' head crowned with thorns. I would then head back to my room to get ready to face my day. At night, before heading to bed, I would spend some more time in there on my knees in silence, thanking Jesus for the day and asking for a good night's sleep.

On one particular night, I lingered. It was quite unexpected. That night I had been asking Jesus to help me with a burden in my heart, a burden I now understand that he himself had put there. It was a burden for souls in need. For many nights previous, I had not been able to sleep as I'd been thinking about those living without hope and purpose. Teenagers in particular.

I was already firming up in my decision to help young people, but three days prior I had watched a movie called *Thirteen*. It was written by Nikki Reed and based on events from her life at the ages of twelve and thirteen. It is a story about longing for love and seeking it in all the wrong places. It details a young person's struggle with drugs, underage sexual behavior, and self-harm.

It had a deep impact on me, having gone through so many similar experiences myself. The change in myself after my breakthrough had been intense, and this movie, along with what I'd seen in my community work, left me feeling restless and with a deep need to do something about the brokenness in the lives of so many teenagers. I honestly don't know what would have happened to me if the phone hadn't rung that day back at home. All I knew was that I wanted to do something to help young people, but I did not know what or even *if* I could do anything.

So I prayed.

I begged Jesus to allow me to become an instrument to help teens like Tracy and Evie in the movie and to provide greater assistance to the young people I'd met on the street. The longing in my heart was real but so was my sense of uselessness, powerlessness, and unworthiness.

I knelt there for hours that night, praying to Jesus in the Blessed Sacrament. At some point, God began to use my imagination to speak to me. As I knelt alone in that small green chapel with my eyes closed, I saw a large cross in the distance. I walked slowly up the hill towards the cross and as I got closer, I could see that Jesus was on it. I knelt before his Cross and looked up into Jesus' face. I could see that Jesus knew I was there. In his pain, he turned his head towards me and looked into my eyes and said, "Rob, give me!"

This made no sense to me. "What Lord? What should I give you?" I had nothing but the clothes on my back. I was just a seminarian.

"Give me!" he repeated.

"I have nothing to give you, Jesus. What do you want?" At this moment in my imagination, I saw Jesus remove his right hand from the *patibulum* (the horizontal beam of the Cross) and reach towards his heart.

He took his heart in his hand and handed it to me, saying, "Rob, give me!"

My heart was broken because Jesus was asking me for something and I did not know what it was, nor did I know if I could give him what he was asking for. I opened my eyes to survey the green chapel, to make sure that I was alone in there. By this point I was drenched in tears and didn't want anyone to see me like that. I got up and put a chair behind the chapel door to keep anyone from coming in. I fell back to my knees at the foot of the Cross.

As Jesus held his heart out to me, it suddenly dawned on me.

I reached for my own heart and held it out to Jesus.

He smiled and suddenly pressed his heart against mine. I was shocked by what I suddenly felt. My heart felt like it was going to burst with love. I wept like a little child as I sensed the warmth of his heart. I became conscious then of how cold my heart had become and, as he pressed his heart to mine, how quickly it warmed up to his.

Jesus looked into my eyes again and asked again, "Rob, give me!"

I knew exactly what he wanted this time. The sound of my heart and his heart were very distinctive, beating as a separate beat. He was asking if I was willing to give up my heartbeat for his. "*Yes, Lord!*" I shouted.

In between my sobbing, I prayed, "Yes, yes, Jesus, I am willing!" At that moment, my heartbeat stopped and all I could hear was one beat. I looked at Jesus and said, "One heartbeat, Jesus, just yours."

He replied, "Listen."

As I listened I could hear that there were in fact *two* hearts, beating in sync.

By this time there was a literal puddle of tears beneath me in that little green chapel. He pulled his heart from mine and when I realized what had happened, I begged him to bring it back. He placed his heart back in his chest and asked me to put my heart back into mine. Jesus then pointed to the bottom of the hill and told me to head back down to let people hear his heartbeat.

"I can't do it, Jesus," I told him. "I want to stay here."

He signaled for me to go down.

I had so many questions. What if my heart went out of sync? I thought I would sin and mess up. I knew I would lose the beat of his heart somehow, even before I got to the bottom of the hill. As I walked down, my tears still flowing but so full of love, I got a revelation that God would be with me. I felt consoled that even if my heart went out of sync with his, he had given me access to the sacraments, and to the Sacrament of Reconciliation in particular, to act as a defibrillator to bring it back into sync.

I still did not know how I was going to let the world know about the heart of God, but I knew that I would spend the rest of my life holding a microphone to my heart, a heart that I would strive, with all I had, to keep in time with the heartbeat of Jesus through a lifetime of prayer and service, encouraged by the body of Christ, the Church, and empowered by God's Holy Spirit.

≈

Once you choose to follow the Lord and his will, the struggle to remain faithful to that call will begin. There have been countless times where I have just wanted to walk away from it all—times when I didn't feel I could fit the mold and other times I felt it was just not worth the struggle, loneliness, and hard work.

As with any commitment, it is not entering into it that is the hardest but being faithful to that commitment even when the enthusiasm and feeling of satisfaction are not as strong as they were before.

When the stress of pastoral work and a lack of feeling appreciated kicks in, it is hard to serve with the same vigor. When people criticize my work and question my motives, and even when they judge me wrongly, I wonder if it is all worth it, but I need to recall that it is not about being successful and understood, but about being faithful to a God who asks for my heart before he does my hands and feet. Recalling the call to be faithful drives me to keep working hard. That hard work is what gives me a true sense of joy and fulfilment in my vocation.

Here are a few things to hold onto as you grow in the confidence, "that he who began the good work in you will carry it on to completion" (Philippians 1:6).

In one glimpse of You
The fire burns within this soul

from the song
"To the Ends of the Earth"

1.   MAINTAIN AND GROW THE VISION. Remind yourself of what God has instilled in your heart and where you saw God taking you. I often open my old journals to read my past conversations with God. Looking back at your previous role models and mentors will also help. Remember why you chose to say yes in the first place but look also to expand that vision. Don't limit God. Understand that God reveals his plans to us one step at a time but know that he is able to surpass all your biggest and wildest dreams. You might have got excited thinking about what Jesus could do with and through your life when you first caught the vision, but in reality, if you maintain the vision and keep being generous with your yes, it is so much bigger than that. Even in my biggest and craziest dreams, I could not have imagined what God has been, thus far, able

to accomplish through my life, and the thing is, I know that the best is yet to come. Dream big and go for the lot!

2. BE PATIENT WITH YOURSELF. You will occasionally lose the heartbeat of God and find it hard to maintain focus at times. There will be moments of loneliness and times when you feel overcome by the distractions of life, but know that there is mercy waiting for you every time you turn back to God. All the great saints struggled and so will you. Be kind to yourself.

3. DON'T FORGET TO KEEP PRAYING. Maintaining a prayer life is also essential. The loss of vocational vision is often a result of a lack of prayer. When we stop praying and being generous with God, everything around us becomes superficial and lifeless. If we want to live in the will of God, we need to be in fellowship with him. When you lose the motivation to pray, try and find new methods and disciplines of prayer. Change the place you pray, the time you pray, or the way you pray. For example, when I struggle to pray, I sometimes use the *ACTSSS* method. I spend three minutes with each of the six letters and their corresponding value.

- **A**doration: three minutes adoring God for who he is.
- **C**onfession: three minutes confessing my sins and my need for him to walk with me every moment.
- **T**hanksgiving: three minutes thanking God for what he has done in my life and the lives of others.
- **S**upplication: three minutes praying for the needs of others.
- **S**ilence: three minutes in absolute silence listening to God speak to my heart.
- **S**cripture: the last three minutes reading a passage from the Bible.

After that, I sometimes journal what I heard God say during those eighteen minutes of prayer.

Other people and cultures have different experiences of God than I do, but music is one way I can begin sharing him.

FIVE

Pastoral Adventures

I didn't know it, but another turning point was coming in my life. While attending a Catholic Charismatic conference in Malta one summer before I entered the seminary, I met Bishop Joe Grech, a Maltese bishop living and working in Australia.

Bishop Joe was the most engaging preacher I had ever met. Young people used to flock to church to listen to him. He was an imposing figure, but he had an approachable face that garnered many young fans. He loved people and had the power to connect to anyone so easily. He could remember names, meetings, and conversations from years before with an effortlessness that I aspired to. The world knew him too; he had plenty of followers beyond Maltese and Australian shores. He was a famous preacher and would often address large crowds around the world. Along with Padre Giovanni, I wanted to be just like him.

I met Bishop Joe in person for the first time during a retreat hosted by the Marana Thà community. I made an appointment to speak to him as I was drawn to his preaching and his inspirational attitude. He patiently listened to me for more than an hour as we paced up and down the small garden of the retreat. He understood the heart of a confused teenager who wanted to serve God but had no idea how to go about it.

"Invest your time and energy in loving people, and God. In due time, he will show you what you are to do,"

Bishop Joe told me. His advice was calming, soothing, and did much to settle my troubled soul.

During one of his public talks on a later visit to Malta, he spoke about his pastoral work in rural Victoria. He mentioned that Australia, though an affluent, first-world country, was one of the most secular nations in the world and in desperate need for priests. I listened eagerly to his talk, as I always did with visiting priests, but then I returned to my studies, not thinking any further on the topic. His role in rural Australia sounded interesting, but it was a world away from where I was at that time.

A couple of years passed, and I was approaching my fourth year in the seminary. All seminarians are required to take a gap year in their fourth year of formation to experience an aspect of life they aren't familiar with. I needed to learn more about the functional church basics and had intended to get it working at a parish in the United States. I found a position as a youth worker in Reno, Nevada, which suited me perfectly. I had been directing my studies and community work towards working with youth, so I couldn't have been more pleased. I packed my bags, bought my plane ticket, and at the last minute, my plans for the United States fell through.

I was floored by what happened.

Just as I was about to leave, an abuse scandal broke out within the Diocese of Reno. This was the first time I had heard about sexual abuse within the Church. I was confused, frustrated, and deeply disappointed. Not that my gap year plans were ruined; no, that was a minor thing compared to the confusion and disappointment I felt learning that a priest would do such a horrific thing to anyone, let alone a young person. I was preparing to lay down my life as a priest, to give hope and dignity to people, and young people in particular. The thought that these men, who were ordained to do the same, would go and do the exact opposite just broke my heart.

I really can't begin to share how shocked and absolutely devastated I was by this.

This was not the Church I had fallen in love with. The priests I knew then and know today are holy priests. The leaders are great leaders. The seminarians I lived and worked with were noble young men, but it seems that I had to discover that just as in any institution, where there are human beings, where there is power, there is corruption. The priests who perpetrated such evil acts lost sight of why they gave their life to God in the first place.

Through their actions they took hope away. They destroyed lives, they destroyed trust, and they destroyed hope.

I am so furious that *anyone* would do anything like this. I don't mean to rant, but it disgusts me and upsets me tremendously that a vulnerable person would be taken advantage of by someone they are supposed to trust. I live my life to encourage our younger generations. Those priests have undone the great work of so many that have gone before them and those that will come after them.

The Catholic Church has lost the trust of so many people because of these scandals. And this is understandable. We have a generation of parents who will not let their children become altar servers. Multitudes have left the church completely.

We are called to be
Your hands and feet

from the song
"Bring Us to Our Knees"

On our part, we have to be so very careful, not only priests but also teachers and anyone working with young people. I cannot even speak to a young person without supervision. Not because I'm not allowed but because I don't want to give the impression that I'm in any way acting inappropriately. My priority is the wellbeing of any young person in my care. We priests need to start from below ground zero to earn the trust back.

I have worked with victims of sexual abuse, and it is just so heartbreaking. I get so angry and so confused that any-one would ever dream of hurting people like this, but by the grace of God, rather than allow this to deter me from my duties, I am *more* determined to be a good and holy priest.

What I didn't realize was the ramifications of the actions of these abusive priests and how they would impact priests that are serving their parishes with honor.

My life as a priest today has been dramatically shaped by the actions of these men who forgot their first love. I have been spat on, verbally abused, and physically attacked just because I am a priest. My heart is heavy, but I live in hope and in the understanding that although profoundly imperfect, the Church still remains the wounded body of Christ, in constant need of mercy and conversion, on a slow journey towards God the Father.

It took me a long time to try to come to terms with what these abusers have done, and part of this process was writing things down. Journaling, as we've talked about, is really good for getting things of your chest and speaking what's in your heart. This journaling about the scandals eventually became the basis of a song called "Bring Us to Our Knees."

Nothing can justify the wrong the Church has done in allowing and hiding abuse, but I know that there is hope. In Jesus there is always hope. My *personal* hope is that we, as a Church, will fall back to our knees and fall in love with Jesus again (see Revelation 2:4).

We need to start by recognizing our wrong, apologizing, and repenting for our sins. However, the reality is that it's the next generation of (innocent) priests that will have to do that.

In general, I have noticed a big change in attitudes towards priests. Whenever I tell people that I'm a priest or they see me wearing my collar in Australia, I often receive looks of anger. People look at me with disappointment. I once had a woman change her seat on a plane when she found out I was a priest. We had struck up a conversation while we were waiting to taxi out where I'd mentioned I was a Catholic priest. She suddenly went awkwardly quiet. It had all been very casual, and I wasn't wearing my collar, but after takeoff she asked the hostess if it was possible to move. Once the seatbelt sign went off she quietly grabbed her possessions and changed seats.

On another occasion, I was walking through the streets of Melbourne soon after my ordination. I was wearing my priestly attire. A man stood in my path so that I could not pass. I tried moving one way and then the other to no avail. He looked me straight in the eyes, glaring at me as though he hated the very sight of me, and then slowly looked down and spat at my feet. His disgust was palpable as he glared at me before walking away.

We can go forward with
a spirit of humility and love

from the video
"Sexual Abuse and the Catholic Church"

I've even been administering the Sacrament of Reconciliation when an angry man sat down and verbally attacked me. He demanded to know why I would still be a priest in and among all this corruption. He raised his voice, getting angrier and angrier at me, shouting slurs and being aggressive, not allowing himself the time to calm down or even take a breath. I had to get up and walk out for my own safety, something I'd never had to do before.

There was another occasion on a Saturday night when we had a youth gathering. It was a pajama and movie party night attended by many people. At the end of the evening, I went in my Superman pajamas to lock the church. To my surprise, there was a drunk man waiting inside the church. He startled me when he jumped up from where he'd been sitting and began to walk aggressively towards me. Even though I was filled with anxiety, I walked towards him in an open fashion, gave him a gentle smile, and held out my hand to shake his hand. That seem to calm him down for a moment.

"Hi, my name is Fr. Rob," I told him, keeping my tone calm and open. I asked him why he was there and we had a little bit of a conversation, but his temper quickly rose again. He started saying that all priests are pedophiles and that the Church is an evil institution. He vowed that he would never bring his children into any church or Catholic school, even though they had been regular Mass attendees for many years.

My heart broke as I listened. There was a lot of pain, anger, and disappointment in his story, and his words held the sadness of his torment.

I apologized for the pain and hurt caused by the Catholic Church. It was all I could do.

People are angry, and I believe that this is justified. I just hope that the next generation of churchgoers will see a

Catholic Church that loves Jesus more than anything else, filled with priests who practice and understand death to self and can be inspired and encouraged by everything that loving Jesus alone means.

≈

As I dealt with my despair at the actions of the priests in Reno, I realized that I needed an alternative to the United States as my gap year was already a few weeks in and I needed to get a position sorted. My mother suggested I try Australia. I was still hoping to go to the United States, but Mum's suggestion had merit. Australia had a need for priests, and I suddenly remembered the talks given by Bishop Joe about that very need.

I sent the bishop an e-mail explaining my circumstances, and he replied within the hour, welcoming me to his diocese. I landed in Melbourne, Australia, two weeks later, and Bishop Joe himself was waiting for me at the airport.

It felt a bit daunting being so far away from home, but it was a great feeling to know that I had at least one connection to Malta here and that I wasn't completely isolated from my home culture or even language. I grew up speaking English, but hearing Maltese every now and then from Bishop Joe was comforting. I had travelled several times before, so I wasn't a stranger to these feelings of isolation, but never had I been so far away from home and for such an extended time. I was to be in Australia for fourteen months! I missed my family almost immediately, but the God I knew and loved was right there with me. I knew I would be okay.

Bishop Joe and I often had conversations about Malta. He had left our small island home and his family to serve the Church in Australia almost thirty-five years earlier. Australia has always been and is still heavily dependent on immigrant priests to meet the needs of the people. The diocese I serve, for example, has eighty-five churches and only thirty-one active priests, eleven of whom have come to serve the diocese from overseas. There was a need here, and Bishop Joe always encouraged me to keep my eyes on serving this need. I did, I still do, and I find great joy in doing it.

I was assigned to a parish in Bendigo, a town north of Melbourne in central Victoria. It was a new country and a new, *overwhelmingly* secular culture compared to what I was used to, but I was drawn to it almost immediately.

As soon as I arrived, I fell in love with the people and how the priests served them. It was very human and holistic, which appealed to my practical nature. They helped sculpt the spirit of the people, as well as the body and mind, from a standpoint that was different from what I had seen in Malta and other parts of Europe. I found it so beautiful. They worked not from above or from any kind of pedestal but from the same level as the people. This, I suppose, comes from the people themselves. Australians don't seem to see the priest as an authority to be elevated but as someone called from among the people to get their hands dirty and serve the people. Because of the lack of vocations in Australia, priests here have to focus entirely on pastoral work, which I think is fantastic. All administration is done by lay employees in church offices, which means that priests can have a powerful impact in their communities.

In Malta, I would often see priests spending hours every day in offices, filling out paperwork and meeting with parishioners who would be queuing outside their doors. People did not do that here. Very few visited the church offices during the week, and they would not come to the parish priest for work references, to authenticate documents, or authorize work on new church building developments like they did in Malta. Instead, priests in Australia spend their entire days visiting schools, meeting families, preparing families for weddings and funerals, or visiting them in hospitals and prisons. Many of those they served were not even Catholic and others didn't believe in God at all.

I had never seen that before.

I grew up in a country where religion was woven into the fabric of every life in every way. The priest served as a pastor but also as a passport photo authenticator, as a job application and retirement home reference, and a parish accountant. It occurred to me that one of the reasons I had initially chafed against being "stuck" in the seminary is that I'd always wished for a church that spent more time with its people. I think I always wanted a church that was ready to encourage its priests to focus entirely on the pastoral needs of its broken and thirsty people. Seeing that in Australia opened my eyes to how much of an impact the Church and community could create together. To my delight, on my last trip home, I could see that Malta today is fast moving towards something that is more community-inclusive.

Parish work in Australia filled the holes in my knowledge of Catholicism, including solidifying the basics such as the Ten Commandments, how to pray the Rosary, and even how to be an altar server.

But the secular society I'd walked into (and this was amid the Church's handling of historic child abuse cases) seemed to be losing interest in the Church. We noticed a severe drop in the number of Australian teenagers and young adults going to Mass in our diocese, and it was a trend reported in other dioceses too. Young people were always a part of the church scene in Malta, in fact it was something I took for granted, but every Sunday in Bendigo, I seemed to be surrounded by a beautiful sea of white hair.

I desperately wanted to see young people come back to the Church. The youth are our future, and everything that I'd experienced up to that point told me that this was where *my* future was. And if they weren't coming to church, then I would attempt to bring the church to them. It might sound ambitious for my pastoral year, but I believed I was following God's will. In my first attempt to do something about the lack of youth, I asked if I could get involved with the local Catholic high school. I made a decision to overcome my shyness and to push my introverted nature to its limits. I began to visit classrooms and spoke at assemblies, and I made sure I was at the school three times a week to speak about Jesus.

It eventually started to bear fruit as I built the trust of the local young people. We started a small youth group that met every week and then organized a youth-led Mass once a month. There was some interest, but because many of these young people were not encouraged in their faith when they got home, I noticed that their enthusiasm quickly faded. We needed more young people so they could also support each other.

I continued to soldier on, and the youth group began to get bigger. Five people at first and then we had eight people. It was slow going, but I knew that what we were doing was the right thing. Faith and community go together, no matter your age. The young needed support as much as anyone.

My agenda was never about getting butts in the seats, but about giving hope to a generation that seemingly did not have God's hand reaching out to them. I visited more schools in the region and even went to nightclubs on the weekend to see if I could strike up a conversation with someone about Jesus. I began travelling across the diocese to different high schools and then eventually to other diocesan schools. If there was a school or club where I could reach people, I went.

I began to be inundated with Facebook friend requests and hundreds of e-mails from teenagers who had been touched by the simple message of faith I was giving. Many spoke about their desire for a connection with God, and others took our connection deeper to talk about their self-harm and suicidal thoughts. I spent a lot of time answering those messages, and that alone could have been the most important thing I did in those early days. I encouraged many of them to get connected with their local parish and youth group, but for many of these young people, they didn't feel their parish was a welcoming place or there was no youth group in their area. It was like something big was missing, but I had no idea what it was.

I loved serving the parish where I was stationed. Yes, the congregation was older, but I was always so inspired by their faithfulness and love for Jesus. When I told them about my desire to see the young people return, they confessed that they too longed for younger people to join them in their worship of God, but they were simply at a loss as to where to begin. Many had children and grandchildren who were just not interested.

Something had to be done.

I asked my parish priest about it, and we spent several hours in Bishop Joe's office brainstorming things we could do to engage this lost generation. It seemed like a desperate situation to me.

I came to see that young people in Australia needed Jesus more than ever.

From where I sat, what I saw was a generation that was disengaged from the importance of family and the community at large. The rise of advanced technology and the need for young people to keep up with everything leads to pressure. To escape, young people lose themselves in entertainment; they perform to fit in, not only at school but also on the way home from school. Then they retreat back to the virtual world in the afternoon as they do their homework and well into the evening.

They get less sleep because they have easy access to their smart devices, and some have even spoken to me of how their only motivation to open their eyes in the morning is to check their Instagram. Too many teenagers spend their time in the virtual reality of social media, a reality that carries only the illusion of intimacy. It seems to me that feeling loved, at times, equates to how many followers they have and how many likes they get, and that the feeling of love lasts only until they post their next image so they can feed off that love again.

I see young people who need to feel authentically and unconditionally loved and accepted. They need to be encouraged and have hope for the future. I believe that young people want a relationship with God, but the problem is that this is not always accessible to them. So many of them do not know where to begin.

I came around to the thinking that we need a Church that can reach out to them where they are, where they live—in a virtual reality—and give them Jesus in that space. The next task was to bring them from that virtual world to the believing community and the sacraments. We cannot expect young people to fill our pews, to come to where *we* are, if we as a Church are not making a serious effort to get into their world and create a dialogue on their level.

I know that I can't win an entire generation, just as Jesus did not win an entire generation himself. He had twelve apostles around him. Some accepted the message; others did not. I do not feel the pressure to convert everyone; I do not necessarily want to change the world. I just want to reach out to one soul at a time.

I want to be just like the little boy who saw a whole beach full of washed up starfish and started throwing them back into the ocean one by one. He was asked by a curious passerby why he was doing that.

"What difference is it going to make?" asked the passerby. "There are millions of starfish on the beach."

The boy held up a starfish and said, "To this one, it will make all the difference," and then threw it into the ocean.

I can tell you that trying to reach one soul at a time is tiring, heartbreaking, and often feels futile, but I see results, and that is what keeps me going. That is what keeps me going from school to school, country to country, stage to stage, open door to open door. Wherever a door opens, I will go.

As time went by, I began to better understand the Australian youth culture. I heard what they wanted, and on that day in Bishop Joe's office, we discussed their needs. They wanted purpose, a sense of belonging, community, and a challenge to do more and *be* more. I wanted to show them it was possible.

My pastoral work had shown me the extent of the Australian millennial disengagement with faith, many of whom were third or fourth generation Catholics that didn't practice any form of religion. In spite of this big challenge, the more time I spent immersed in this culture, the more I felt I belonged. This is what I wanted to do: I wanted to spend the rest of my life reaching out to people who were disengaged from Christ and the Church. Even today, I feel as much at home surrounded by a group of atheists, agnostics, and the un-catechised, as I do surrounded by faithful parishioners during Sunday liturgies. And it wasn't that the disengaged Catholics were unwilling to find their faith. It was that their parents, grandparents, and even great-grandparents would, at best, only enter a church to "hatch, match, and dispatch," as I mentioned earlier. They would use a church to get baptized (often done just to get into a Catholic school), get married, and eventually, buried.

There was often no faith support at home for these young people, so even when they accepted and wanted to live out their faith, they were often met with a lack of support and encouragement in the place where they spend most of their time and among the people they love and trust the most.

I prayed long and hard for wisdom and guidance to create a space where these young people could meet Jesus Christ and grow in a relationship with him, with the Catholic community, and be sustained by his Word and sacraments.

With the help of Bishop Joe that day, I formed a youth ministry program called Stronger Youth for the diocese of Sandhurst, recreating the youth ministry in Malta that had helped me so much. Stronger Youth began as a small weekend retreat and today has grown to be one of rural Australia's largest Catholic youth ministries. Creating this ministry just seemed so right. I was trapped in the worst kind of darkness as a teenager, and that wonderful youth group in Balzan helped pull me out. I wanted Australian youth to have that kind of safe place too.

Growing and staying strong in faith is exhausting and so countercultural these days. We get hundreds of teen-agers attending our retreats and rallies, and at the end of these events, they often enthusiastically sing the praise and worship songs all the way home. They get home and talk to their parents and friends about the fun they had and feel joyful and encouraged in their faith. It feels like their hearts are overflowing with the love of Jesus.

But almost without fail, the feedback I've had indicates that this enthusiasm starts to fade by the end of the week and is all but gone by the end of the month. Given the extraordinarily large geographical size of our diocese, these teens do not have the opportunity to meet up with their faith-filled friends too often. They are very much isolated until the next rally or retreat. It breaks my heart because

I know how difficult it is to keep our faith alive without having others to spur you on in your faith journey. Having other faith-filled young people constantly around who can support you and help you to persevere when you feel like giving up is so important.

That's why Stronger Youth also uses Facebook, Twitter, and other social media sites. We try to keep a strong online presence because we do know how hard it is to stay connected. Australia has such vast, open spaces that a young person on a cattle farm is bound to feel isolated, as much as someone who is close to their parish but without family support for their faith. Online environments can help minimize the disconnect.

The reality is that we need each other and we need the youth. We need a thriving youth community to build the next generation of healthy and devoted adults.

Today, Stronger Youth serves thousands of young teens and adults through a series of retreats, concert rallies, parish-based youth groups, seminar days, school outreaches, youth-led Masses, and leadership formation opportunities. It has been a wonderful (and sometimes heartbreaking) journey, but I am constantly amazed as I witness so many young people discover their faith in Jesus.

Building this program and gathering more young people has gone some way towards alleviating the problem of distance and holding onto their faith when separated from the community, and it helps that technology has allowed us all to connect in powerful ways. Support is just a text, direct message, snapchat, or tweet away.

≈

My gap year flew by in my rural bush parish, so when Bishop Joe invited me to stay in Australia after my gap year ended, I gladly accepted, despite the pain of being separated from my family. At many points throughout my gap year I found the pain of separation almost unbearable. I missed my parents, my brother, my sister, and my friends. The homesickness I feared had hit with a vengeance, and I missed Maltese culture and food. I longed for my mother's home-baked pasta and Malta's traditional meat and fish dishes. I missed the sparkling blue ocean and taking trips on the water to fish and swim and snorkel. I was born in the embrace of the Mediterranean Sea, and being in a land-locked parish was a new challenge for this water-loving priest! And Australia, for such a hot country in summer, can get very cold in winter.

When I was back home for a visit before committing to Bishop Joe's invitation, I went to visit the vicar general of my seminary to discuss my future. He was actually some-what relieved at Bishop Joe's offer. He told me that it solved a problem that he had at the back of his mind: where to place me once I was ordained. He wanted me to work with young people and saw that I had the gift to do so, but he didn't think that Malta would provide me with the right opportunity to reach my potential.

I know now I was seeing God's hand in all of this.

At the time, there was a pang of sadness that I wouldn't be making Malta my home, but I knew the vicar general was right. I'd seen the value of the Stronger Youth ministry, and I knew that God's hand was in this work.

Once I decided to move back to Australia, I had to break the news to my family. It was hard news for them to take, but they knew that I needed to follow what I believed to be God's call. My parents had heard of all the good work that I was doing and had even come over to Australia to visit me once, but it didn't stop the many tears that were shed that day when I said goodbye to my family at the national airport south of Valletta.

I might live across the globe from my family now, but I haven't cut them out of my life, and I didn't back then either. Being a priest or a seminarian doesn't mean you cut all ties with your past life. I called them every week, and I still do to this day. Some days as I studied, we would set up a Skype call. We would talk for a while, catching up on all the news, but then we'd just hang out. I'd leave the video call running as I sat at my desk going over my study notes and my family would have the camera and screen set up as they watched TV together. We would occasionally talk, but mostly we'd just enjoy each other's company, even though we were thousands of kilometers away. I'm so grateful for technology as it means that I can stay close to all of those who matter to me.

I still find great comfort in talking to my mother for hours. We can chat about anything, from things happening in my life to the musings of my heart, and of course, I love hearing about all things happening with her and at home. I also make it a point to try and return home every year, even if it's just for a few days. I love my work, and I love how my family still gets to be a major part of my life. God didn't give me good. God gave me best.

≈

When I returned to Australia after saying goodbye to my family in Gudja, I thought I knew the culture well enough, that I understood it after my gap year, but slowly, as I made Australia my home, I began to see how different Australian culture is from Maltese culture. Australia is much more of a secular culture and Malta is much more of a religious culture, by which I mean, religion is part of everything in Malta. It's tied up in every single element of Maltese life. Although the Church significantly impacts the Australian people through its hospitals, schools, and charitable organizations, most are indifferent to the Church and its moral voice. As I was growing up, most of the pastoral work of the Church was within church walls in Malta, while most of the work in Australia is outside the walls of the church in the community. Many of Australia's country churches are almost empty of young people, but city churches have plenty of young people because that is where folk who immigrate into Australia usually start—in the cities.

I'd completed my seminary gap year, but I still had a couple more years left to go in a seminary environment. I ended up in the heart of Melbourne, which is different to rural Australia in almost as many ways as Australia is to Malta.

≋

There were times when I felt disengaged from Australian culture, I can't deny that. I could not make sense of everyday things like Aussie Rules football, which Victorians seem to go nuts for. Initially, there were many nights where I cried myself to sleep with a deep sense of loneliness. It eventually got easier, but even today, though I am happy living in Australia, I hate missing out on the marriages of my family and closest friends. It saddens me that when I return home to Malta I do not recognize and am not recognized by the children of those I was brought up with. But in spite of that pain, I know that I made the right decision to move here. Every day, my determination to make a difference grows.

I saw more and more that I belonged here to start a dialogue with an indifferent, atheistic, and agnostic society. There were many things I did connect to and love. The beautiful beaches (of course!), the open spaces, and the wonderful roads that stretch out and meander across the countryside. I loved the passion and brotherhood of the Sandhurst clergy and the support they showed me as a seminarian and young priest. The laidback nature of the Australian people was also something that relaxed me and drew me to this great southern land of the Holy Spirit. The people here have such a great attitude towards hard work and yet they know how to take time for themselves too. There's no doubt that the Australian beaches, terrain, people and clergy are very different from Malta's, but I quickly grew to love this place and make it my home. The Catholics I worked with were incredibly supportive and enthusiastic, and I was always encouraged by them in my work as a seminarian and later as a priest.

I finished seminary training in Melbourne before I took up my post in Sandhurst. The culture in the seminary in Carlton was very different from my Maltese seminary. The jokes were much more tame for a start! We had ensuites and very nice rooms in a beautiful area of Melbourne known for its great food, coffee, and multiculturalism.

I found myself with a new group of people who had spent the last four years getting to know one another very well. I was nervous at first, but that faded as I was made to feel welcome very quickly. The study was not as intense as it was in Malta, but I'm so glad that I got involved and studied hard because it showed me a new perspective of the Church in Australia and what my work was to be.

I knew that my approach and attitude had to be different if I was to work here, that I would have to learn to converse with a culture that knows no religious language and practice. I had to learn to work with Australian culture and strip back some of my Maltese mindset but without compromising on the truth as Australians have a very different approach when it came to talking about moral issues such as abortion, euthanasia, the treatment of refugees, and speaking about God in government-run institutions. It is forbidden, for instance, to promote matters of faith in public prisons and state-run schools. I needed to learn how to listen, sit with people, and patiently construct the way I acted, the words I spoke, the songs I sang, and the clothes I wore so I could fit in and have an impact.

I'm grateful that I had my music in that time because it was a great link to my evangelization ministry. It allowed me to speak the language of the people without fully understanding the culture and show them what I was about in a way that was non-threatening. For instance, when I visit prisons and state schools in Australia, I'm reminded that it's forbidden to preach about Jesus. I was not to come across as *trying* to convince anyone of my faith. I'm so grateful I have the gift of music. What I'm able to do is introduce myself as a Catholic, sing a few pop songs, and then mention that I also have some original songs. Music is just so powerful that way.

My travels throughout my time in the seminary also led me to serve some Aboriginal communities. Spending time every year with the original Australians and participating in their daily lives gave me an even greater understanding and appreciation of this country and its history.

My fellow seminarians helped me there too. I took the time to get to know them, learn a few Aussie slang words, attend the confusing Aussie Rules football matches with them, eat their food, and watch them interact with their families. I especially loved seeing them with their families, even though I would get wistful pangs missing my own family. But all this helped me understand Australian culture a little bit more.

The seminarians and I prayed together and supported one another in our studies. I suppose that is an advantage of living in a community of people who are on the same sort of journey. We also played sports together. In Australia, we had an inter-seminary soccer tournament. Every year, all of the seminaries across Australia would play soccer against each other. Our Melbourne team never won a tournament, but it was a great way to connect with other seminarians. Those tournaments were lots of fun as we got to hang out with seminarians from all across Australia. I even started to see the cultural differences in people from Sydney from those in Melbourne and other areas too. It was surprising in some ways, but then again, Australia is a very large country. You can get around the main island of Malta in less than an hour, but it takes many days to get from one side of Australia to the other! It's no surprise that the people are different in the major cities.

Living in a community like the seminary was a means for me to learn how to love and respect those around me as well as serve them even when stress was high and patience was running low. I learned how to look out for my brothers when they were going through difficulty, even when I felt I needed attention myself. I suppose it is a reflection of what priestly life is like in the parish and in our pastoral ministry.

Sometimes we would succeed at living in harmony and at other times we would fail miserably. On more than one occasion, I had the opportunity to let go of an argument but would stubbornly persist until someone would leave feeling angry and upset. Learning to put others before ourselves was very difficult, but all difficult things are worth persisting with when you know that you'll become a better person for it.

So many times, for example, I would buy washing powder for my clothes and find that other seminarians were using it without my permission. That would frustrate me to no end. Eventually, I found that the best solution was to hide my washing powder. At other times the busy work of studies and life would make us less sensitive to the needs of each other. On one occasion, I remember one brother wanting to talk to me about something that was weighing on his mind, but I was too busy. I pushed him away with promises of talking later.

We never got that talk.

A few days later, he announced that he was leaving the seminary. I was devastated. He must have been dealing with a lot of pain the day he asked for a chat, and I put him second to my own needs. How I wish I could have been less preoccupied with my own world and more sensitive to his need to sit down and talk that day. I wonder sometimes what would have happened if I had made the time for him that day. Would he have left the seminary? I don't know the answer to that, but I can tell you that today, he is a very happy and successful businessman who still revels in the presence of God.

Other than the challenges of living together, my time in the Melbourne seminary was like living a normal life. We lived right next to the street that I think serves the best coffee in Australia. We would spend lots of time having coffee and, on the occasional evening, having some beers together too. It was a good way to distract ourselves from the sometimes exhausting routine we carried on day after day. It also provided plenty of laughs and opportunities to meet the community, as on the odd occasion, we would bump into someone who would recognize us and be surprised that future priests were allowed to enjoy a good beer and a good time.

The final years of my studies went by in a flash, and now, I look back at my seven seminary years (eight, when you include my gap year) with great appreciation. I made lifelong friends and learned what it means to live in and selflessly serve a community. I use those skills all the time in my parish community, living with other priests, and on the road when travelling with my band. Seminary life also helped me appreciate the need for accountability and service. It is all too easy to become isolated and not be accountable to anyone in a rural ministry such as ours.

≋

I was ordained in Malta in 2010 and then came back straight to Australia. The happiness I felt as a newly ordained priest was tempered by the sudden death of Bishop Joe, who came to my ordination but died only weeks later of a blood disorder.

I was devastated.

I had become very close to him since I moved to Australia, and he was a caring father figure when I missed my own. We were supposed to go on holiday together, a vacation to celebrate my ordination and our hard work, but he died the day we were to head off. Grief is a funny thing. It didn't really hit me until the day of his funeral. It got to a point I could not stop myself and began crying uncontrollably.

I suddenly felt so very alone. He was the only Maltese person in my diocese that I knew of, and he also was a great mentor. He taught me how to love and serve people authentically and enthusiastically, no matter the place, sinfulness, sexual orientation, or self-righteousness. He loved and cared for people indiscriminately, and I wanted to do the same. He was my friend.

I became determined to carry on his legacy of helping young people recognize the love of Christ and that they have a place in this world not as the Church of tomorrow but as the Church of today. I was able to help do that through running our diocesan youth office.

Just before he died, Bishop Joe appointed me as an assistant parish priest to St. Brendan's Parish in Shepparton. This was a young, multicultural, and dynamic parish with a primary and secondary school. I was loving my work celebrating Masses, weddings, and funerals. I ended every day feeling happy and fulfilled in the work I did, and it was obvious to me that the people appreciated it. It was like Bishop Joe had left me a parting gift with that wonderful appointment.

Ten months into my appointment at St. Brendan's, my parish priest was called to another position in New Zealand. Not even one year ordained, I suddenly found myself running one of the largest parishes in the Sandhurst diocese as well as the continuing task of running our diocesan youth office and undertaking the occasional interstate and international speaking engagement. The parishioners and staff stepped in and offered a lot of support, but things were to become a lot more challenging and difficult one Sunday night.

At 9 p.m. on January 8, 2012, I got a call from Notre Dame College, the secondary school where I was chaplain. One of our students, a fifteen-year-old girl, had just killed herself.

No seminary and theological formation can ever prepare you for a moment like this, and believe me, we study heavily for challenging situations in the community like this. It's exactly for these situations that we spend hours and hours immersed in topics like psychology.

I walked into the house where just a few hours earlier, this beautiful teenager had hanged herself. The family was inconsolable, and I was lost for words. I stood there with my soul screaming and crying inside, wanting to take away some of the pain, but I felt useless and in the way.

The grieving mother came over to me and hugged me, thanked me for being there, even though I was in shock, bewildered, and feeling utterly useless.

But for the first time since my ordination, what I was seeing was how just the presence of a priest felt like a wonderful consolation to a family in a time of pain and desperation, even though I personally felt superfluous. I spoke no words, did nothing, but for the family I represented a God who cared—one who stood there amid their pain.

I visited again the next day, the following day, and the one after that. My workload intensified in the community, as the girl's death had affected more than her family. Her school friends and fellow students were grieving, and so was the wider parish. As one of the representatives of that community, I spent hours talking to her peers, her friends, and those poor souls who blamed themselves for her death. It was a horrific couple of weeks leading up to her burial, full of grief and stress, but I had to be present and available to those who needed to talk. As a representative of God, I was much sought after for advice and solace in that time.

I had no idea that this was just the beginning of a cycle of tragedies in that one town that would lead to a dark situation for myself.

Less than a week after the burial, on the first of February, another tragedy struck the town. I received a call to attend to another family whose sixteen-year-old daughter had just committed suicide.

Again, I sat with the devastated family for hours and helped them bury their little princess too. And again, I had the conversations with friends and family and spoke words that I hoped bought consolation and comfort. I spent many hours in prayer during this time, asking God what else I could do to help. It never felt like enough, and so I pushed myself to work harder for my community.

A couple of days after the second burial, on the eleventh of February, I was notified that yet another sixteen-year-old had passed away. This time, I had to go and visit a family whose daughter had accidentally fallen off a horse and died.

I could not believe it. My heart was raw and broken after two suicides, but I just had to put my head down and attend to the situation, even though I was overwhelmed with despair and working long hours to support three grieving families and a shocked community. I was newly ordained, alone in a large parish, and inexperienced. I had no proper support structure, as my greatest support and friend, Bishop Joe, was now gone. I felt myself starting to struggle during this time of darkness.

During my homily at the third funeral I wept. I wept, and I just could not stop weeping. After the funeral, I kept weeping, and the next day I wept again. I could not stop crying, and I could not face people. I would perform my duties and celebrate Mass but hide from people after that. I told myself it was just a phase, but it kept getting worse. I was stressed, anxious, depressed, and scared. I was over-worked, exhausted, and suffering.

Something had to be done.

For a long time after the funerals, there was still a lot of grieving within the families and within the community. I wanted to be there for the people and the town that was suffering, but I just could not. I was burning out.

≈

The aftermath of a death can lead to so many different reactions. Some people blame, others act out. I've found that reactions can be exacerbated after losing someone to suicide, as a lot of questions are left in their wake. How should we react to such a loss? We can blame ourselves, blame them, or even blame God or the community. These are all understandable and natural reactions to grief. We are also left with a lot of "what if" questions. For me, all I know is that God is mercy. In my experience, those who take their own lives are not always in a position to make a rational decision. Sometimes they have lost a sense of control or are struggling under the weight of personal conditions. To them, it may seem like they have no options. I know that their actions are not right, nor are they justified, but surely God is mercy. God knows their pain.

Those who are left to grieve need support. They need to talk about it.

When we are faced with suicide, the pain doesn't only affect those who died or want to die but also the survivors, those who loved and cared for that person. There is no easy way to grieve someone who has died from suicide. And nobody experiences grief the same way. Some may experience it physically and others emotionally through reactions such as a sense of numbness. Others may succumb to shock, guilt, or uncontrollable sadness or anger. Others may just deny that it ever happened. In time, some can come to find a sense of acceptance.

Accepting suicide is made harder by the fact that there is a stigma associated with it. It can isolate us from our community and friends because we are ashamed; we don't have the right words to explain what happened. We're also confused emotionally because there's no time to grieve the loss of the person before people begin searching for answers. Who do we blame? Usually, there's no one to really blame except the person who took their own life, which can lead to a sense of abandonment and betrayal. Rejection even.

We always try to understand why. Perhaps that is the true nature of grieving.

But this is why it is so important to seek the right support; preferably before such an event ever takes place. If you know someone is struggling, then reach out. If necessary, seek professional help. Talk about the pain with family and friends. The same goes for grief after the fact. Pull together those who you love, reach out, and talk about it. Try to live in the moment and cherish those around you. Express your pain in creative ways such as journaling, praying, and meditating, and find an outlet outside the house. Take a walk or get some exercise—anything to help you express your anger, loss, and grief in a safe way. Also—and this is the hard part—try not to hold onto any guilt. Allow yourself a holiday and some time away, even a bit of fun. You are not betraying the memory of the person you lost in doing so. Come back home, reestablish your routine, and then push on. Look after yourself and those around you.

≋

A few weeks after the third loss, a new parish priest was appointed to St. Brendan's, and upon his arrival, I took a couple of weeks off to rest.

I went to stay with a priest friend of mine, Fr. Chris Reay. Fr. Chris and I could not be any more different. He was laidback and I was intense; he had a slow work ethic and I was a workaholic. I worried about everything while nothing ever seemed to bother him.

He was always socially awkward, or at least, I thought he was. One time we were on an plane. He was in the aisle seat, I was in the middle seat, and there was a young woman in the window seat. Curious about the view, he leaned across me and looked out the window but did not notice that the woman thought he was looking at her. She kept staring at him awkwardly, but he had no idea because he was too captivated by the view outside! As he stared intently past her, her gaze turned uncomfortable when he uttered loudly, completely oblivious to her discomfort, "How absolutely beautiful!"

I had to turn to the woman and explain that he was referring to the view outside the window and not her. Not that she wasn't charming!

I learned a lot from him, and two of the greatest lessons were not to take myself too seriously and not to worry about what others think of me.

"Don't worry about what others think of you," he would say, "because most of the time they don't."

It was a true and good thing to keep in mind and the best encouragement I could ever receive as a young priest. When I got put down by the public for voicing a certain teaching or opinion or when I was scared of the bishop moving me to a different parish, he always reminded me to trust in God.

He also encouraged me to take greater care of myself. He could see that I was burned out and suffering under the weight of grief and exhaustion from the tragedies in my community.

With his help, I made a commitment to look after myself, and I was able to pull myself out of the dark place I had been sinking into. I made a commitment to daily meditation and Adoration of the Blessed Sacrament. I visited a naturopath, a personal trainer, and eventually made a commitment to take time every month to rest. I even got a dog and named him Gozo, after one of the Maltese Islands, to remind me of home.

I began a strict regimen of diet and exercise. I ended up getting rid of all sugar and processed food in my diet and made time to exercise every day. Today, five years on, I feel healthier and fitter than I have ever been my entire life.

Somehow, throughout my seminary formation and pastoral zeal in my first year as a priest, I had neglected my physical and mental health and, eventually, I paid the price for it. I didn't take care of my physical health, I wasn't managing my depression symptoms, and I had bottled up too much of my own feelings in my desire to serve others.

This is reminiscent of priestly expectations in years past. Priests invest their energy and time in the souls of others, often at the cost of their own spirituality and humanity. We begin with a great enthusiasm, like a jar overflowing with water. We give water to people out of this overflow, but before we realize it, our jar no longer overflows, and we start to give people our own supply of water. Eventually the jar runs dry, and all we have left to give is ourselves. At our worst, we break off pieces of the jar, giving people the broken pieces because we are conditioned to give no matter the circumstance.

It was fourteen months since my ordination, and I was feeling broken, out of water, somewhat disillusioned, and hurting terribly from the tragedies in my parish. To this day, I am so glad that Fr. Chris noticed this in me and took me under his wing.

Depression is something that affects the whole of your life. It is not just this feeling of sadness. It is an internal pain that cannot be explained. A fire that cannot be extinguished. An evil that makes you feel evil when you know you are not evil. It makes you feel bad when you did nothing to feel bad, and that feeling bad makes you feel both evil and bad. It compounds in and of itself. All sense of confidence suddenly disappears and there is confusion, disappointment, and a deep, deep sadness. Life seems pointless and not worth living, and you start to think that you are burden on people. You might even have a feeling of tiredness and sickness and just want to move out of existence. You can't work or socialize, and you can't make sense of your emotional pain. Things that were once joyful now mean nothing. You're unable to concentrate enough to pray and to love and care. You feel like a fraud.

I felt all of those things. It took me right back to when I was a confused and hurt teenager, which only made my despair worse because I thought I'd moved on from those feelings. I knew I had to find a way out of this. I wasn't going to wait for a phone call this time. I had to make the move myself.

I had to set boundaries and routines in order to cope with my sadness and depression, which I still suffer from occasionally. I make sure that I complete my daily discipline of exercise and prayer. I make sure I am creative and use my mind to write songs and work on projects like this book. I meet up with people even when it's the last thing I feel like doing.

I've also had to recognize my limits and to learn to say no when I felt that I was too busy.

People don't always understand the reasons why I decline certain requests and invitations. My office receives more than four hundred invitations per year to speak and sing all around the world. I have had to find the means to employ people to look after all these bookings so that I can focus on my ministry at hand and myself, too. This year I spoke to more than 200,000 people at events all around the world. I use social media and YouTube to keep connected with those in my ministry, and I'm amazed at what God has done with a mess like me, but I know now, I have learned my lesson, that there are times when I have to say no.

I've been called lazy and selfish, but at the end of the day, if I don't look after myself by first knowing my limitations, then I am no use to others or to myself. Ultimately, it is my responsibility to make sure that I can be fit and strong to serve God and others for as long as I can. I think back to my early days in the seminary where I wanted to help everyone all the time, but I know that it's not always possible. I need to be healthy if I'm going to spread the Word and share a relationship with Jesus.

I have also been criticized for putting too much emphasis on physical health, but I believe that physical, mental, and emotional health are all connected. Ever since I started exercizing regularly and eating properly, my mental health and emotional health have improved dramatically. I have more strength, more confidence, and more ability to be disciplined in other areas of my life. I think it's made me a better priest.

If we are to serve God effectively, we need to look after ourselves and recognize that we are human beings in need of gentle care. This challenging time at the beginning of my priestly ministry helped me understand that I needed to learn how to find peace in what God saw me to be and not my own or others' expectations of me.

I learned to create the habit of investing in my mental and physical health on an ongoing basis. I learned, in essence, that to help people authentically, I needed to not only look after my relationship with God but to take responsibility for the care of the temple of the Holy Spirit: my body. 1 Corinthians 6:19 says, "Do you not know that your bodies are temples of the Holy Spirit, who is in you, whom you have received from God? You are not your own."

≈

God loves us. He loves our souls, but he also loves our minds and bodies. He loves our humanity—our strengths and weaknesses, our gifts and talents—and asks us to be his witnesses by the way we look after not only our souls but also our minds and bodies.

I quickly got my balance back after my visit to Fr. Chris and returned to my parish, youth, and travel ministries. I love what I do. I love serving God, and I love serving people and pointing them to Jesus Christ. I have been a priest for seven years now, and as time goes by, I am growing to understand, appreciate, and love the priesthood. There is no greater honor than to point people to Christ through the Word and sacraments.

Looking back, I am amazed at where God has brought me. It all started with a nervous and awkward conversation with a charismatic bishop in a small retreat garden in Malta. Years later, I am serving the very people he had a heart and passion for. I know now that it was all in God's plan. That meeting, the cancelled trip to the USA, the gap year in Australia, and the eventual decision to stay here were all his design. Before every step on my journey, I did not know where I would take the next step. I just walked. I just sought God and trusted. I had to trust and hold on to him, as I stepped out in faith and left my family for a far-off land. I walked in faith and not by sight when I reached out to the younger generation outside the church walls. I had to trust and hold on when I was left alone in the parish and had to deal with the pain, suffering, and questions that came with the suicides. And then there was the return of my own darkness and depression. This time it was different from the abyss I faced as a teenager. This time, even though I was in deep pain, I knew I was not alone. I knew that there was hope. God was with me, and I had the support of God's people around me.

I love to serve God and his people. I often feel inadequate and out of my depth, but I will keep walking, often blind, holding on to Jesus, committed to working hard to glorify God and God alone. My path is determined to help our young people find a home in a loving and welcoming Church, which is often perceived as not being so. I think a key factor when feeling burnt out or depressed is to reflect and, more importantly, trust in God. This is the time to keep it simple and focus on your key reason for being.

1. GO BACK TO YOUR FIRST LOVE. Find a quiet space to read and reflect on this Bible passage. Read it twice. Once out loud

for your mind, and a second time in your mind for the ben-
efit of your heart.

> You have persevered and have endured hard-
> ships for my name, and have not grown weary. Yet
> I hold this against you: You have forsaken the love
> you had at first. Consider how far you have fallen!
> Repent and do the things you did at first. If you
> do not repent, I will come to you and remove your
> lampstand from its place. (Rv 2:3–5)

2. **PRAY.** In the first part of the chapter I talked about the Church
losing its focus and purpose. You and I are called by God
primarily to love, not to serve. Our serving God becomes
then a consequence of loving him. We can too easily get
busy doing things for God and forget to spend time with
him, getting to know him more and staying in love with him.
Think about your journey with God, where you began and
where you are. Write down in your journal or think about
where you have climbed and where you have fallen. You can
try writing a letter to God, asking for forgiveness for choosing yourself over him and for the grace to seek him first in
your life. Pray that you will find the strength and determination to keep your eyes on God, trusting and loving him
above all else.

3. **TRUST WALK.** "Even though I walk through the darkest valley, I
will fear no evil, for you are with me; your rod and your staff,
they comfort me" (Ps 23:4). With your first love by your side,
even the darkest valleys and the highest mountains become
possible to track. It becomes a journey of walking behind
God with your arm on his shoulder. Often you will not know
where the next step will lead you, nor will you know if you
will have the strength of will to make it to the end. Your only
consolation will be that Jesus is walking right there before
you. You don't need all the answers as to where he is leading

you; you only need to know that he will never let you go. Ask Jesus to lead you. Surrender your present and your future to him. Let Jesus know that you do not need to know all the answers but only to know and understand that he will be with you, guiding you every step of the way.

4. OUT OF THE DARKNESS. Sadly, grief and loss are part of the human experience. Loss is inevitable, and grief is a natural human response to loss. But we have the hope of our first love, and we know that God is strong enough to carry our burdens (see Matthew 11:30). We can surrender our hurt to God because he cares for us (see 1 Peter 5:7). We can find rest in the Holy Spirit (see John 14:16). In the storm of grief and pain, God can be our anchor. We can rely on the community of the Church, dig deep into the truth of the Word, and find hope knowing that even here, God has not left our side (see Hebrews 6:19-20).

Every time I get in front of people, whether it was my first crowd of two hundred or in front of 200,000 people at World Youth Day, I am always scared. But I still perform; I do it scared.

SIX

Receive the Power

I am an introvert. Maybe it is because I was bullied as a child or because I never felt good enough as a teenager. Maybe it is simply the way God created me to be. There is absolutely nothing wrong with being an introvert as long as your introversion does not slow you down from pursuing your God-given dreams.

Many people find it hard to believe that I am a shy introvert when I tell them. I spend a lot of my time, almost every day, on stage in public, speaking to crowds all over the world in front of live audiences as large as 500,000 people. Once on stage or in front of the camera there is no evidence that I am shy or that I would rather be alone in my room with my little dog Gozo, binge-watching one Netflix series after another.

In actual fact, I do spend most of my time alone. I always seem to be at airports, presbyteries, hotels, some church or chapel praying, the gym, or my office preparing talks, songs, and writing scripts for my weekly YouTube series. I can't handle crowds, parties, and social events. I get confused, lost, and anxious and am constantly thinking of ways to get out of such situations. Even though I do not let it stop me from visiting parishioners, I can imagine few things worse than knocking at strangers' doors for pastoral visits. My anxiety levels skyrocket.

Before I step onto a stage to speak to people, my heart beats so hard and fast that I sometimes worry I will pass out or go blank once I get to the stage. My legs shake and my stomach aches. I pace up and down backstage, as I pray that God's Holy Spirit works in and through me. I just want to hide, to be left alone. I don't feel able or competent enough. I am so often scared—but I do it scared!

I will never forget the first time I was invited to speak on a microphone in front of a medium-sized crowd. I was seventeen years old. I had been attending the Marana Thà Catholic community for almost a year at that point, and Dr. John asked me to share my conversion story with two hundred people at a meeting. I said yes.

When I got home, I suddenly realized what I had committed to and was overcome with a feeling of nausea and panic. Five days before my debut on stage I lost my appetite. Three days before I was unable to sleep, and one day before I kept running to the bathroom under pressure from my nerves. By the time of the meeting, I was a total nervous wreck.

Every part of me did not want to go ahead with it, but I knew I had to.

You see, a few months prior to being asked to speak in public, I had a dream.

It was a daydream during one of my daily Mass visits. I was sitting alone, hidden behind a protruding wall towards the back of my parish church, the Parish of Mary Immaculate, Mother of the Church, in Ibrag, Malta. I had a blocked nose and a bad cold, so I sat away from the rest of the people so as not to spread my illness.

The people in the church had just offered each other a sign of peace as I sat hidden in the corner. I knelt down in silence as the priest held up the Body of Christ and proclaimed, "Behold the Lamb of God who takes away the sins of the world, blessed are those who are called to the Supper of the Lamb."

Out of nowhere, and all within the matter of a split second, I came to a deep realization that the Eucharist was real. I couldn't explain it, but in that pure moment, I knew that I knew. I began trembling as I knelt there alone. Then, immediately following that miraculous moment, I saw a picture in my mind of myself with a microphone talking and preaching to thousands of people. It was so clear! I suddenly knew that I would one day stand on a platform and talk to people about Jesus.

I opened my eyes, and people were queuing up to receive Holy Communion. As I walked back to my place after receiving Communion, I noticed that my nose was no longer blocked. In fact, my cold had disappeared completely. A miracle? I believe it was. It also served as a confirmation from God that he would fulfill the vision that he instilled in my heart that day.

I walked out of the church with a fire in my heart, but I had never spoken in front of a crowd before, nor could I imagine myself doing it without some miracle of God removing the intense fear I had of public speaking. I knew that one day I would be able to overcome my fear of addressing a crowd, but that was something I thought was way off in the future.

Not even two months had passed since that intense vision and here I was, asked by Dr. John to speak in public. I said yes without hesitation. God was moving quickly!

The time had come.

It was a Friday evening prayer meeting at Gattard House in Blata l-Bajda, a small town a couple of kilometers outside Valletta. I sat in the front row feeling sick to my stomach at the thought of speaking to the crowd behind me. I had planned a speech and had a paper in my pocket, but my mind kept blanking out. I could not remember what I had to say and how I was to say it.

Then Dr. John announced my name: "I would like to invite Rob to come up here and share his testimony with us." People applauded, but I was way too nervous to acknowledge their open hearts and waiting ears.

I stood up and my legs were shaking. I smiled, but I was holding my hand close to my face just in case I had to suddenly throw up, which was a real possibility, by the way. My stomach was doing somersaults.

I made it to the microphone, but that is the last thing I remember.

The next thing I recall is sitting back in my seat. I was confused and terribly embarrassed. Mark, my friend who had been there for me since the first youth meetings, was sitting beside me. He was telling me not to worry and that it would all be okay.

"What would be okay? What just happened?" I asked him in confusion.

Apparently, I stood before the microphone and completely blanked out. I had stared at the microphone and nervously laughed like a fool. I stood there, awkwardly, for just under a minute until Mark ran onto the stage, took me by the arm, and led me back to my seat.

I could not believe it! What a disaster.

As you can imagine, I could not wait for the meeting to be over so I could run home and cry. Walking out at the end of the meeting was a nightmare, as many in the congregation tapped me on the back and shoulders, commended me for my effort, and told me not to be too concerned. I did my own walk of shame to the door and went home and cried.

What was going on? I saw it so clearly in the vision only a few weeks earlier. I was going to be a confident communicator, God had shown me, but there was no evidence of that in my first attempt at public speaking. It was a wreck.

Six months passed in a blur, and Dr. John approached me to give it another go. The thought of embarrassing myself like that again made me cringe. I so desperately wanted to say no, but I couldn't. I said yes.

I went through exactly the same symptoms as the last time. From loss of sleep to shaking and the feeling of nausea, I was plagued by them all as though it was the first time. I took my place in the front row of the Gattard House hall and waited for Dr. John to call me up. With the same trembling and nerves as before, I walked in front of the microphone to the sound of a great encouraging applause from the congregation. It buoyed my spirits, but . . .

I opened my mouth to speak, and what happened? I completely blanked out *again*. Disaster version two was in the making. I stood there with my mouth open, but no words to show for it. The people kept clapping to encourage me to speak, but the words would not come out. I had to walk off the stage, defeated once again. I felt so discouraged.

A year later, I was asked to sing a song during a Mass. I had just started playing the guitar and thought that I would give it a go after my two previous failed public-speaking attempts. A year had passed since the last time I stood on a stage, and my dream of one day holding a microphone and preaching to the masses was still burning in my heart. Plus, this time I had a guitar to back me up.

What could possibly go wrong? This was it, my moment to shine.

I played the C chord to begin singing, and because of my nerves, my voice pitched two semitones too high. Another train-wreck! Disaster version three. I kept singing for a couple of bars, but then I noticed the look of horror on the faces of the congregation. I stopped suddenly, fell to my knees, and cried. Why was it so hard? Why? If God wanted me to do this, why was he not helping me? I knew I could sing, but no one there that day could have possibly known that from my disastrous performance.

I had a dream, a God-given dream. I had no evidence for the fulfillment of that dream except the Word spoken into my heart on that day almost two years previously. I held onto that Word and was determined not to let these disasters and my fear stand in the way. I was going to make my way to the stage, and music would lead the way.

≋

Sometimes God instills a dream into our hearts, a dream of liberation, opportunity, or healing, a dream of unity or breakthrough. In the physical world, there is no evidence for this promise; in fact, you'll have everything and every-one around you telling you that it was a lie, that it's too hard, and that you must have misunderstood the dream. In the absence of all evidence, this where you need to brace yourself and step out in faith. The author of the letter to the Hebrews nailed it when he said, "Now faith is confidence in what we hope for and assurance about what we do not see" (Heb 11:1).

Faith is not just believing that God will follow through; it is also stepping forward as though he has already done it. I knew that God would eventually deliver on his promise. I *would* proclaim his Word in public one day, but right then it seemed like an impossibility.

I did not wait for God to give me the courage but repeat-edly stepped forward in my fear and disappointment. I failed over and over again, and for a while it seemed that with every foot I put forward, I took ten steps back. I kept embarrassing myself every time I took to the microphone, but I could visualize myself preaching to multitudes and did whatever it took to press into that. I did not want to miss out on this God-given dream while waiting for God to take away my fear. I was fearful, I was scared, but I did it in spite of my fear—I did it scared.

≈

The first breakthrough came two years later.

I was twenty-one years old and had been caring for my old friend Daniel. I was in my first year of seminary, doing everything I could for Daniel while still studying, but he was going downhill. Severe muscular dystrophy can often take young men in their late teens and early twenties, and Daniel was fading fast.

He fought for as long as he could, but eventually, my friend died. His tired and overworked heart finally gave out. After seeing his lifeless body, his spirit gone to God, I was moved to write my first song, "Run to Jesus," but that was only after I cried my heart out. My grief was overwhelming at the time even though I felt such relief that he was no longer in pain. He was my closest friend, and I was going to miss him, but I was glad he was finally free of his disease.

I sat in my car for hours after he passed, just thinking about Daniel and praying. When my head was clearer, I grabbed a notebook I had in the glove compartment and wrote down a few words. It was the first song I ever wrote.

When I got home, I shut myself away and put a simple melody to the words, eschewing food and my studies, and drove back to Daniel's house to have his parents listen to the song.

To my surprise, his parents asked that I sing it at his funeral. Even though I was honored by their request, I was terrified at the thought of singing in front of a crowd of people, but I agreed to do it. He was my friend, and I would not let them down.

That day, and who knows, maybe it was because of the other emotions that accompanied my fear, I was able to sing in tune. I could not believe the amount of people that came to thank me for the tribute after the funeral Mass. I was so happy that I was able to honor Daniel in this way, but I was also grateful to God for breaking through my fear on a day when I really needed to be focused and clear of mind.

Daniel's parents and his sister approached me after the service and asked me to record the song in Daniel's memory. They offered to pay for the best producer and recording studio in Malta. I was initially hesitant, but eventually I booked the studio and recorded the song, along with another two songs I had written since Daniel's death.

I released it as an EP, and to my surprise, it became a best-selling single in Malta!

Once the EP was recorded, I printed a few CDs and gave them away to Daniel's family and to my family and friends. Other people wanted copies, and so I decided to put the record out for sale. I printed hundreds of copies, and then thousands. I just could not print them fast enough. From there, I got contacted by newspapers and magazines for interviews, I was invited to make radio and TV appearances, and then I was asked to sing at a few parishes, youth groups, and religious and fundraising events.

Because I was already a seminarian by then, I would use my days off to attend some of these invitations. All of a sudden, I was a reluctant national celebrity—Malta's "singing seminarian."

I kept my public appearances simple as I was still very uncomfortable in front of people and I was grieving for my friend. Daniel hadn't been gone for that long, and I missed him. To make it easy on myself, I would plug my guitar into the amplifier and sing the same three songs which I had perfected. I would not speak except to answer questions. I had discovered a formula that worked, and I was not going to deviate from that for fear of blanking out again.

Somehow, my music got into the hands of a small record company in the United Kingdom that offered me a record deal. A year later, I travelled to England to record my first full-length album. This album was called *Closer* and was released in 2006. The *Closer* album opened new doors for me as my music got regular radio play in Malta and the UK. I was invited to do radio interviews and give small concerts across Malta. As the attention for my music grew, we got the band who I made the recording with together and organized a public concert. We booked a small venue that seated three hundred people, and tickets sold out within a couple of weeks.

Our precious Daniel,
run to Jesus

from the song
"Run to Jesus"

Closer was to be the first of six records I have released to date. My desire is to love and serve Jesus first, but music has given me the opportunity to reach such a wide audience. As I studied over the years, I kept writing songs about the people I met and their struggle to find God. A year after *Closer* was released, I had enough material for my second album, which is called *What a Day*. A couple of weeks before my ordination, I released my third album, *Reach Out*. At that point, I had not given a concert since my first album and many people were asking for another live performance. We sold out three concerts this time and recorded the fourth album, *Reach Out Live*, which included new songs and live versions of various songs from all of my previous albums.

Then there was the *Divine Mercy Chaplet*. I had discovered the Divine Mercy prayer when I was in the seminary in Australia. It is a powerful prayer of intercession asking God to help and have mercy on the world he loves. I wanted more people to know about this soothing prayer and got together with some friends to turn it into music.

After being a priest for a couple of years, my understanding and appreciation of the liturgy began to mature, so I decided to write some music for the Mass. I wanted young people to be able to enjoy playing and singing for this great event. This was my "Glorify" Mass Setting. Then in 2015, I wrote the album *Something About You*. These are songs about my own search for God and understanding of what I have learned about God and just how little I know about him. I am currently working on my next album, but I'm not sure where that one's going just yet.

I could not have imagined how many people would be blessed through the music I wrote. I have received countless e-mails and letters from people around the world who have been inspired to pray and worship God through these albums. I've got a few strange e-mails too! Some people use my music to put babies and even *dogs* to sleep at night. One mother even gave birth to her child while playing and meditating on my recording of the *Divine Mercy Chaplet* instead of taking an epidural!

≈

Even though my music was doing a lot of the preaching for me, I did not appear in public for a couple of years after my initial flush of fame as I was focused on my seminary formation. I was happy with my choice of the priesthood and committed to the seminary.

While I studied, I had the opportunity to write more songs, so I didn't feel as though I turned my back on music, nor did I forsake it for the Church. Songwriting served as a form of spiritual journaling for me. I would write about my encounters with and desire for God. I wrote to shout out loud what I heard in the secret space of my heart. Initially, I never intended to record the songs I wrote, as to publish these songs would be reveal the depth of my heart and make myself vulnerable. Later, I came around to the decision that I would record the songs with the intention of letting the world hear my heart beat for the heart of God.

Interestingly, it was at the time that I released the *Run to Jesus* EP that I really started to reconnect with my father. Our relationship had been strained after I chose to enter the seminary, but I knew that my father was always proud of me. However, the first time I really saw pride in my father's eyes and saw his acceptance of who I was and what I'd chosen to do with my life was the day I got a record deal. He wanted to tell his friends and contacted radio stations to get some airplay for Daniel's song. He would talk to all of his employees and customers about me and did everything he could to promote what I'd done.

I know that he was proud of me at other times, but that was the first time I could really see it, and that meant more to me than the record deal and even the music itself. My dad has been proud of me ever since and has made a point to show it. He's my greatest supporter today. I love him with all of my heart, and the distance between Australia and Malta only makes me appreciate him more today. My dad has Parkinson's disease now, a degenerative disorder that affects motor movement, yet he is still strong and an inspiration to me with his hard work and determination. I see a lot of myself in him: his personality, his drive, his determination, his risk-taking, and even his business mind. His life has not been easy, and the same for my mother, too. I think all I ever really wanted was to make them both happy, and I knew back then that I had.

≈

After my initial success I'd kept music on the backburner in order to study, and then the time came for me to take my pastoral year in Australia. While I was working at the parish in Bendigo, I was given many opportunities to speak and sing in public, and looking back from my first stage appearance where I'd completely blanked out, I could slowly begin to see the fulfilment of God's promise. Music, which had been pushed down my list of priorities while I studied, became an important factor in reaching Australian audiences. It was a tool that I started to use more often.

One of my earliest invitations to play in Australia was to perform in a country town seven hours' drive from my parish. I packed up my guitar and overnight bag and drove for those seven hours to play for ten people! As I mentioned earlier, music was a great way to share the heart of Jesus, so I also began a weekly Adoration night where I would play music and sing as people adored the Blessed Sacrament. Soon, other people in the community began to find out about this, and it didn't take long before we had a full church every week. In conquering my introverted ways when I was looking to reach young people, I started playing at schools and occasionally travelled the two hours to Melbourne to play at youth groups.

I was seeing that music and youth were working really well together, and it became the genesis of how I could run my ministry in such a way that attracted some people back to the Church.

In October 2007, one year after I first arrived in Australia, I received a phone call from the World Youth Day office in Sydney. World Youth Day is a big international Catholic event started by St. John Paul II. This event attracts crowds as large as four million young people from across the globe to share a week of prayer and catechesis with the pope and other young pilgrims from around the globe. In 2008, it was Sydney's turn to host the biannual event.

The person on the phone that day from World Youth Day was Fr. Peter Williams, the priest heading the event. I had never heard of Fr. Peter. He explained that a copy of my *Closer* CD had appeared on his desk, and he asked if I would be interested in singing for the pope and to a live audience of half a million people at the twenty-third World Youth Day in July the following year.

I could not believe what I was hearing. I said yes immediately.

With the permission of the Bishop of Sandhurst, I flew up to Sydney to Sony Records headquarters to meet up with the team who were heading the musical part of the World Youth Day event. They showed me their schedule, which was intense, as they had planned a lot of work for me to do. They sent me to singing lessons to hone my voice, and then they asked me to write and record several songs until they found the right ones for me to sing. I worked hard in the studio until the right songs were found, and then I practiced hard and prayed for months so that I would not embarrass myself in front of the extraordinarily large live audience and the estimated one billion television viewers. As you can imagine, my nerves were strung pretty tight!

The day finally came, and I made my way through tight security to the back of the stage at Barangaroo in Sydney. The energy in the place was unbelievable. You could hear the singing and chanting and see flags representing every country in the world being waved enthusiastically through a veritable sea of people. It was chaotic, stirring, and inspiring.

For someone who doesn't like crowds, I was having a hard time, but the wonder at what I was seeing was so powerful, that I was able to push my social anxieties to one side.

The 500-strong choir arrived backstage soon after me. Their reactions were not too different from my own and ranged from excitement to horror as they looked at the massive crowd from the back of the stage. There were a good number of choir and band members literally throwing up with fear. I think that sort of thing is contagious because my breath was getting shorter and shorter and I was on the verge of a panic myself.

Backstage with me was Australian pop idol Guy Sebastian, who was to sing with me during my first song. The second song I was to sing alone on a minor stage in front of a smaller crowd of 200,000 World Youth Day pilgrims.

In my desperation, I asked Guy what I could do to calm down. We said a prayer together and he told me to visualize the microphone as the ear of Jesus and when on stage to gently sing to my audience of one. What great advice! I could do that. I felt calm as I prepared to go and sing my heart out to Jesus.

We got the one minute stage call and were ushered towards the stage. Just as I was making my way onto the stage, somebody grabbed my arm. It was the person in charge of the Sony team for World Youth Day. "Rob," she said, "we have invested so much in you; please don't embarrass us."

Well. I suddenly lost all focus and walked on stage with a shortness of breath. I forgot about singing into the ear of Jesus, as what she just said roiled through my mind like a tidal wave. I looked at the crowd in front of me and my knees nearly buckled, but I pushed my fear back, took a deep breath, and gave it all I had. I was scared, terrified even, but I did it scared, and it was a success.

My life was never the same from that moment. I knew that if I could survive that momentous occasion, I could survive anything. From that point on, I could face any crowd and stand on any stage. It was like the chains of fear that were holding me finally broke. They had no power over me anymore.

≈

That performance on World Youth Day put me on a world stage. In the days following that massive event, I got flooded with requests to perform at Catholic events all round the world in places like England, India, Qatar, Indonesia, the Philippines, the USA, and Canada. The first invitation I accepted was from Fr. Tom Rosica, a priest who headed a large Catholic television network, Salt and Light TV, in Canada. I flew to Toronto during my summer holidays (their winter, so very cold!) to be interviewed by the network and to give a couple of concerts.

From there, I went on to the United States and then to India. I was speaking to auditoriums full of young people—12,000 people in Los Angeles and 14,000 in India. I could not believe it. I sang and spoke about the God I loved, and those teenagers were listening. They could not get enough. There were conferences in England, concerts in Malta, youth rallies in Indonesia, and parish missions across Australia.

I performed for thousands of people, and at these events I saw thousands of young people give their lives to the Lord, with many choosing to serve him through the priesthood and religious life.

What an absolute miracle to behold.

I was seeing God's promise being fulfilled before my eyes. I spoke to countless teenagers that summer. I had no idea that this was just the beginning of something greater than I could ever have hoped or imagined. It was all too easy to get lost in the fulfillment of my God-given dream. People were paying attention to what I had to say. We were selling records, and the invitations to speak and sing across Australia and the world were coming in faster than I could fulfill them.

Doing it scared: performing before 200,000 at World Youth Day in Sydney, Australia, 2008

Music, my beloved music, which I once thought I'd have to give up, has played a vital role in my ministry. My role as a priest is to proclaim Jesus through his Word and sacraments. Music is the language of the heart, and I use it to proclaim God's Word to the hearts of God's people. I am not a performer or an entertainer but an evangelist. We are all called to be evangelists, to spread the Good News to those around us. People are desperate for the truth of God's unconditional love and promise of salvation. This freedom is theirs but they need to know where to receive it.

> "Everyone who calls on the name of the Lord will be saved." How, then, can they call on the one they have not believed in? And how can they believe in the one of whom they have not heard? And how can they hear without someone preaching to them? (Rom 10:13–14)

In the middle of all the hype and attention back in 2008, I got a call from one of the heads of the World Youth Day team. Her name was Bonnie. Bonnie had noticed all the attention I was getting and all the amazing opportunities that were opening up for me. She was happy for me, but she said to me, "Rob, it seems like you have a choice. You need to choose whether you want to be a pop star or a priest." She was quiet for a moment, and then she said, "I hope you choose to be a priest. A holy priest."

These words cut straight to my heart. I hadn't realized how quickly pride could enter into the most noble of intentions. I was doing God's work after all, but I had to take a step back to make sure that it would not stand in the way of the more important call over my life, to be a Catholic priest. I know that I'm lucky because my bishop and diocese encourage my work as both a priest and a musician, but I didn't want anything to interfere with my integrity as a priest.

I am grateful for Bonnie's words that day, as they serve as a constant reminder to me of my vocational priorities. I am first a follower of Jesus Christ, then after that I am a priest. Only then comes my call to share God's love through the proclaimed Word and music.

You need to consider your own dreams, and what God asks of you. Pay careful attention and be aware of your integrity.

1. I HAVE A DREAM. God is a giver of dreams, and any dream he gives, he will watch over to fulfill, but the fulfillment requires obedience and courage. He has a dream for your heart as he had for Joseph in Genesis 37. This dream was met by a lot of opposition, as will yours be too. But with a spirit of obedience and determination, and not letting fear have the last say, it will come to fruition. "The one who calls you is faithful, and he will do it" (1 Thes 5:24). What dream has God instilled in your heart? If you do not have one, ask God to sow a dream into your heart.

2. IT IS COSTLY. The fulfillment of a God-given dream costs a lot. It takes blood, sweat and tears. Not many are willing to pay the price of perseverance, failure, and getting back up again when knocked down. Jesus had a dream. It cost him his life. Abraham had a dream, and he had to hold on and trust for what seemed like an eternity until he began to see it come to be, only to be asked by God to sacrifice the very fruit of his fulfilled dream (see Genesis chapters 12–22). Are you willing to pay the price to see God fulfill the dream placed into your heart?

3. IT'S NOT ABOUT US. A God-given dream involves us but is never about us. It is all about fulfilling God's purpose in this world. When it becomes about us, it drains us of joy and freedom rather than fill us with it. "Not to us, LORD, not to us but to your name be the glory, because of your love and faithfulness" (Ps 115:1). As this dream grows in your heart, and as you work hard to work with God to give birth to this dream, pray for humility. Surround yourself with people who will remind you that it never was and never should be about you but only to give God the glory.

Performing on The X Factor Australia *was a great experience, but I had to choose: Did I want to be a performer or a priest?*

SEVEN

The X Factor

I woke up at 5 a.m., feeling terrified and excited and thinking that this could be the day that would change my life forever. Today, I was reaching secular society in a way I'd never attempted. I got dressed and drove the two-hour journey from my parish in Shepparton to the Melbourne football stadium where the audition was to take place.

When I arrived, there were thousands of excited contestants queuing up, all being handed audition number stickers. I was greeted by one of the producers who handed me my sticker and escorted me through the doors to a backstage area packed with people doing warm-up vocal exercises and production video cameras. Some people were visibly more nervous than I was, with some people crying and some people pacing, while others were confidently flaunting their eccentric personalities and guitar skills before the cameras and other contestants.

I sat with a couple of close friends who were there to give me moral support as I waited to be interviewed. Not long after that, I was to be called to the stage to audition for the seventh season of *The X Factor Australia*. I was about to stand before Dannii Minogue, Chris Isaak, James Blunt, Guy Sebastian, and a live audience of five thousand screaming *X Factor* fans.

The time came, and then it was my turn to walk out onto the stage, and even though I had performed on the World Youth Day stage, I still had to do it scared. I was shaking on

157

the inside, but I tried to portray a calm and collected persona on the outside. I was greeted with a gasp as I walked out to face the judges and audience wearing my black shirt, priestly collar, fitted jeans, and Converse shoes.

Australia is such a secular country that many in the audience had never seen a priest wearing a collar before except in movies and on the news. They did not know what to think or what to expect. The audience listened in a hushed silence as I had a conversation with the judges—it was so nice to see a smile of recognition on Guy Sebastian's face—and then I began to sing a Swedish House Mafia song. As if woken from slumber, the audience suddenly came alive.

Fr. Rob Galea performing
"Don't You Worry Child"
by Swedish House Mafia

The X Factor audition

This is the power of music. It can transcend thoughts, ideologies, cultures, languages, and religion. Once I completed my song, I saw from where I stood on the stage that the first person in the audience to give me a standing ovation was a Muslim woman wearing a hijab.

I stood there in awe at where God had led me.

Can you believe it? A hopeless, young, scared, introverted, talentless Maltese teenager brought up in what is possibly the most Christian nation in the world was now standing before one of the world's most secular audiences, boldly displaying his priestly attire and talking about his love for Jesus and the Catholic Church.

Do you ever get those split-second moments where you suddenly wonder how you got to be standing where you are?

That was certainly one of those moments for me. But there was more to it than that. I had a sudden realization of the climb I'd endured to get to where I was.

When I encountered Jesus at the age of sixteen, I wanted to share his love with the world. My idea was quite simplistic really—just talk about Jesus and what he did and many people would realize their need for him and turn to him. I began talking about Jesus at school and when I was out with my friends, I'd write songs about him and share those songs online, and later I'd perform on different stages around the world. I had an immense joy with Jesus in my life and I just had to tell the world about it. I did that for years without understanding the cost I had to pay for it to really bear fruit. And what was that cost? My life. Not once, not twice, but a surrender of all that I am each and every day.

What does this even mean?

Even as a seminarian, I hadn't quite understood it. To share the Gospel is not only about the words we speak or the way we act. True evangelization is becoming a perfect icon or reflection of Jesus. In order to be a perfect reflection, it means we have to hide, to get out of the way of the mirror. As a Christian, a priest, and an evangelist, people see me. When I walk on stage they see my face and my hand movements, they see my clothes and hear my voice, but all that is an instrument for them to hear a heart that is poured out for Jesus. I am not afraid to let my individuality and my humanity shine, but only in as much as it will draw those who want to listen to a heart that loves Jesus more than anything else—not just when I am on stage but every day of my life. This generation is desperate for people who are not afraid to be all that God created them to be but that, while living out their uniqueness, are pointing to Jesus through their words and life of integrity.

≈

After I had sung my song, I had another conversation with the judges on *The X Factor* stage. James Blunt spoke about how he did not know what it was but that the hairs on his neck were standing on end. It was not the song, he said, but what he felt while I was singing it. I looked into Guy Sebastian's eyes and they were welled up with tears as he said how much he loved hearing me sing. It was the first time I'd seen him since we'd performed together on the World Youth Day stage, and I think I was feeling just as emotional as him. Chris Isaak stood up and said that as a Catholic, it made him want to return to the Church and get back to Confession. Dannii Minogue said, "You had us from hello."

I don't think there was anything extraordinary about my singing performance that day. It was not the skill and technique that they and the audience connected with, but I believe, even though they may not have realized it, that they somehow participated in my encounter with my audience of one as I sang the song. They heard a heart that was beating for Jesus.

I walked off that stage, not thinking how good or successful I was but in absolute gratitude to God for allowing the audience there, and on national television, to have a small glimpse of his love for them. God used me—my actions, mannerisms, musical talent, clothes, and accent—as his instrument of reflection. It's the reflection from which I continuously seek to hide so that my pride and selfishness will not obscure God's reflection.

This is not to say that I have it all worked out. I am still prideful and seriously imperfect and sinful, but I have learned not to be afraid of my humanity and my uniqueness in bringing Jesus to this world. This world is distancing itself from the transcendent and, in turn, from God. God is becoming too far-fetched for many people, inaccessible and unreachable. This was the case in the Old Testament and that is why the Father chose to send his Son into the world. He became one of us, wore the same clothes as us, had the same mannerisms as us. He was like us but without sin. A man of perfect integrity, a man in perfect love with the Father.

This is where I want to be.

I want to be my true human self with the people of this world and for the people of this world, an accessible reflection of the true Light of the world, but I pay a price for that. I cannot afford to be afraid of my humanity: my hobbies, my strengths, or my weaknesses. I also need to be focused on living a life of integrity, and that requires a constant death to self: resisting temptation, choosing to put others before myself, making a daily commitment to the sacraments and to prayer, and investing in, and allowing myself to be invested in, by the believing community.

The reality is that the Church, that is, you and I, need to go where people are. We need to understand that the first thing that people will connect with, both young and old, may not be the transcendence of God, but the humanity of the person communicating the message. The Church needs to become a role model. We know the reasons why it has lost its credibility as a role model and that is why the next generation—our generation—needs to rise up and create a *new* generation of role models who young people want to be like: real, human role models who are committed to Jesus.

There is a young generation of faithful Catholics, as well as priests, that is recognizing this need to let their humanity shine: Catholics who excel in their sport and their art and music and are unafraid to give glory to God through it.

From a champion cricketer bold enough to invite his team-
mates to join him in prayer before every game to the tat-
too-covered young musician who unapologetically speaks
and sings about Jesus during her pub and club gigs. From a
nun who regularly and relevantly uses social media to doc-
ument her everyday, human life, including both victories
and trials, to the priests I myself hang out with at the gym.

One Saturday afternoon, I went to work out at a local
rough-tough bodybuilding gym. It just happened to be the
gym's thirtieth anniversary. As soon as I walked in, the
owner asked if I would bless the gym. I was in my gym
gear ready for a workout, so I hadn't been expecting it, but
I agreed to do it if he provided me with a cup of water to
bless. He handed me a glass of water, stopped the music that
was playing throughout the gym, and made an announcement over the loudspeaker for all members to come to the
front reception. I could not believe it. He announced that
the priest would be saying a prayer and that he would like
us all to join with me in prayer on this special occasion. I
made the Sign of the Cross and began praying.

Although many there did not quite understand what
was going on, they all joined in. After the prayer, many
commented that they hadn't been to church for way too
long and that it made them think about their faith again.
Others never thought that God would be interested in being
in and blessing a gym.

Catholics need to be in the world but not of it. While
you are called to be in and reach out to this world, which
is in desperate need for Jesus, you also need to recognize
the temptations and trials that may come from being this
close to the edge. But the reality is that the Church *needs* its
disciples to wander out into the deep, close to the edge.

I want to be on the edge because people are falling off the
cliff and they need Christ's disciples to reach out and pull

them from danger. However, to be at the edge you need to be honest with yourself and with God. You need to commit to daily prayer and the sacraments and have other faithful people around you who can speak into your heart when you yourself get too close to the cliff edge. At the edge, the struggle and the temptation are real.

Auditioning for *The X Factor* was an edge-of-the-cliff moment for me. To be surrounded by people for weeks on end who knew nothing of Jesus and the faith and to be exposed to a national audience who could have turned on me at any moment was terrifying. Yet being there allowed me to reach out to people who would have otherwise never seen or met a young Catholic priest whom they could connect with. This allowed people to see the Church in a new light.

With the judges' stamp of approval, I got past the *X Factor* audition and made it through to bootcamp: two weeks of training with one hundred other contestants. It involved days of intense vocal training, filming, and televised singing challenges. By the end of the first week, and after a series of elimination challenges, there were twenty-four of us left. I was so happy to be there.

The producers and crew were giving me a lot of attention. They and the national Australian press were saying that I had a good chance of winning the show. I liked where this was going. Can you imagine what good I could have done for Jesus with all this attention and exposure? I felt excited and honored to be in such a position, but deep down I could sense that there was something not quite right. I acknowledged the feeling but put it aside as I trained.

While I was there I could see God work through me. The judges were speaking out about their own faith in God, and the other contestants were opening their hearts to me about the difficulties in their life. Some "in the closet" Christians secretly came out and told me that they believed in and loved Jesus. They didn't want the others to know because they didn't want to be judged or treated any different, which was something that I found heartbreaking. Plus, they thought that it would allow them to behave as they pleased without being considered hypocritical. Whatever they decided in how they chose to represent themselves, I was there if they ever needed to come back to acknowledging Jesus.

One day, just before one of the singing challenges, I stepped out in faith. The contestants were moved into a theater, surrounded by lights and cameras, and we were about to be culled from fifty to twenty-four in just a matter of minutes. There was a deep sense of fear in the room. As we waited for the judges to enter, I stood at the front of the hall and shouted out to the other contestants that I would be going over to the side of the theater, just out of the way, and that I would be praying with anyone who wished to join me.

The entire group joined me!

I prayed for peace, for calm, and that Jesus would give us the courage to bring out our best. As I took a breath to continue my prayer, another contestant chimed in to speak their prayer to Jesus, then another, and another, and another two after that. Wow! It was such a beautiful prayer experience and one of the most memorable moments of my time on *The X Factor.*

People embraced one another, wished each other the best and took their seats to begin the challenge. After the challenge, one of the contestants approached me and told me that he was overcome by a deep sense of peace as we prayed. "What was that?" he asked.

"That was the presence of the Holy Spirit," I told him.

He reached out his hands to me in a prayer gesture and said, "Do it again." He wanted his next "Holy Spirit high." I prayed for him. This time tears streamed down his face. An hour later he asked me to do it again and again two hours after that. He had encountered the love of Jesus, and it filled him in such an expansive way.

I was so grateful that God was allowing me to serve him this way, but again, I had that odd sense once more—and this time I knew what it was. I had done what I was sent to do, and I needed to move on. I was on the edge of the cliff reaching out to many who had been lost and forgotten, but I also knew the limits of my ability to deal with the pressures of fame and constant attention, especially when weighed against my obligations to my parish and community.

After days of prayer, a few conversations with Fr. Chris Reay, who was my spiritual director at the time, and at last a peaceful heart, I decided to leave the show.

Many people could not understand my decision to throw away such a great opportunity to evangelize, and I can truly understand their argument, but God knows that I did not want to risk losing my soul, and my peace, for a few opportunities to make the Gospel more relevant and approachable. Matthew 16:26 says, "What good will it be for someone to gain the whole world, yet forfeit their soul? Or what can anyone give in exchange for their soul?"

My call to be a saint, to be like Jesus, and to be holy and my vocation to the priesthood, which I love dearly—these are not things that I would ever risk losing.

≈

Music is a very big part of my ministry. Out of all the tools I use to reach out to people, music seems to have the greatest power. I don't know what it is exactly, but whenever I preach using music, people listen. They understand. They connect.

I don't know if you remember the first album you ever bought. I remember mine. It was the album *Smash* by The Offspring. The first track is a spoken track called "Relax." The twenty-five-second track finishes off with a powerful short statement which rings so true: "After all, music soothes even the savage beast."

Music does have that power. Just think of David and King Saul in the first book of Samuel. King Saul was oppressed by anger and a demonic spirit. He often became depressed and inconsolable until David was brought in to play music for him. The Bible says, "Whenever the spirit from God came on Saul, David would take up his lyre and play. Then relief would come to Saul; he would feel better, and the evil spirit would leave him" (1 Sm 16:23).

I see this happening so often during my work as a priest. At a youth rally or school assembly kids can be distracted, talkative, and disengaged. As soon as I pick up the guitar and play music, I see their eyes open wide and they are ready to receive, ready to listen. Music encourages participation and community.

This week I got to speak to 23,000 teenagers in a big stadium. It was the first session of a large conference. Some of the young people were feeling awkward and out of place as it was their first time at an event like this. I got them to sing and dance along to a few new songs and a couple of familiar pop songs. The atmosphere in the place was suddenly on fire. People were laughing, smiling, and interacting with others they did not know. I was later sent several Instagram videos of busloads of teens singing the same songs and doing the same dance moves on their way home that night.

A similar reaction to music happens at funerals too, although on a much more serious note. Often, particularly after a tragic death, those grieving are not in a state to take anything in. There is too much pain and too many questions.

But once the music begins, there is a sudden peace in the room and people are ready to listen and to pray, and some can even start to release their grief if they'd been numb. I'm sure that you can think of circumstances in your own life where music has soothed the savage beast in you. I'm so grateful for music. Music has opened doors for me that I otherwise not have been able to go through. It has given me the opportunity to work with people and groups that I otherwise could not have. I have been able to share Jesus through music in state prisons, hospitals, nursing homes, Protestant churches, at inter-faith gatherings, pubs, and nightclubs. I've collaborated with famous DJs and pop stars and that has allowed me, as a priest, to perform on platforms and share the Word of God in places that otherwise would not allow it, such as in clubs, where the music often glorifies drugs, sex, and money. I was able to bring a song that speaks about human dignity and love and the need to stand strong in adversity to several clubs across the country. In collaborating with pop stars, I got to preach about surrendering to Jesus to people on their way to work and in their homes, on secular radio stations, on televisions across Europe, and in Australia through reality television.

There's a million people
with a broken heart
Everyone is looking for change

from the song "Dominoes"
feat. Ira Losco

Music gave me the opportunity to put out into the deep, and to get to a section on the edge of the cliff where the Gospel would otherwise not have been heard. But it's not only music that we can utilize to preach. We need to use every means possible to share the good news. People need to hear the Gospel in a way that they can understand and take in. Sure, we need to use traditional means such as preaching in our churches and religious TV and radio stations. But what about those who won't step into our churches? Those who won't visit our Catholic blogs and YouTube channels? What about those who cringe at our Catholic TV and radio stations? Or how about those who do not attend our Catholic schools? People are being lost to secularism. They have never heard the Good News being preached in a way that impacted them in any kind of authentic form. We need to be restless, passionate, and relentless in our thirst and pursuit for souls.

St. Paul was relentless. Look at the letter to the Romans, or any of his writings for that matter. He wanted to preach. He wanted to tell people about Jesus. He wanted to be in Jerusalem, in Spain, and in Rome. He was one-track-minded. He was not going to rest until the world heard about Jesus.

This is my attitude too.

I will use conventional methods to talk about Jesus, but I will use everything else I can get my hands on too. I will use social media, filmmaking, music, and body art, and I've even designed some cool apparel that people can wear. All that I am will seek to shout God's fame!

This shift to technology is no gimmick. The reality is that teens are spending more time in front of their phone and computer screens than anywhere else. Facebook, Instagram, and YouTube are their communities. That is where they are being influenced and formed and the Church needs to be there. We need to set up our pulpits and lecterns on Snapchat and Netflix. This is why I decided to produce a weekly YouTube vlog. Every week I talk to thousands of people through my words and filmmaking. I always have a camera at hand and a drone in my backpack. I try to make it real, relevant, and authentic to my life, which I pray and hope will connect with others out there who can find hope and direction through what I create.

Using social media allows me to connect with people on a human level. People ask me why I don't post holy pictures but I post gym selfies. Point people to Jesus, not to yourself, they say. This is a valid point, but I find that people need to be pointed to God *and* those who are his disciples. They need role models who they want to be like, act like, and believe in. A role model needs to be human, strong, and even weak, too. If we are not out there being real, they will find other role models whom they aspire to be like. A good role model can show the sort of strengths they aspire to but is also unafraid to broadcast their humanity.

The Church needs to set up shop in the virtual world, as I've found that is where to reach the next generation of believers, but this will never replace the credibility of its physical presence. My weekly videos and music are played in schools across Australia, Europe, and North America, but that can never compare to the influence I have on my local schools, youth ministry, and community. I do travel a lot, but the vast majority of my year is spent working day in and day out with the parishioners, students, and young leaders within my diocese. All that I do in my other means of evangelization pales in comparison to the ordinary, day-to-day ministry of hanging out on school grounds during student lunch breaks, attending our parish and diocesan youth meetings, giving parish liturgies, and meeting people on a one-to-one basis.

Because of our ageing clergy and significantly increased regulations in child safety around adults, the priests in our diocese are becoming less and less present in the lives of our teenagers. I am no way blaming anyone in the community for any safety precautions, but it is just so sad to hear that priests are actually afraid of hanging around with young people now. They don't know what to say. They don't know what they can or cannot do.

My close friend Fr. Chris Reay used to see me speaking to young people on the school grounds when he visited me. "I wish I could do that in my secondary school," he told me once, "but they would never come up and talk to me."

I challenged him to walk through the grounds during the student lunch break every day and to say hi to anyone who made eye contact with him. He was never one to shy away from a challenge, and so when he next heard the lunchtime bell he headed out and just walked slowly but confidently across the grounds. It was terribly daunting at first, but after a few days the first person came to say hello. The next week another few came to talk to him, and within a few months he could sit on a bench in the middle of the playground, out there in the open, and the students would come and chat with him. Through that he gained the confidence to visit some classrooms, and during school liturgies, he would start to know some of the kids by name and ask them to help out. They did so joyfully. Fr. Chris gained credibility not through his gifts, talents, or special abilities but simply through being present.

We have the greatest influence on people when we are present in their lives: a mother and father present for each other and their children, a catechist present every week to serve the disinterested confirmation class, teachers present every day at school, and the priest present in the confessional, even when no one ever shows up. Jesus travelled much and reached out to many, but he was present to his twelve apostles. He invested time and energy in them. He formed them to become leaders and men who loved God above all else.

My Stronger Youth leaders are my disciples. My band members are too. They are the people that I invest in week in and week out with sometimes what seems to be little or no results. However, with them it is not about the results, but about being an ongoing icon of Jesus. I run leadership days and Bible studies for them, and sometimes nobody shows up. At times like this, I do wonder whether it's worth the effort. I tell myself I could be speaking to thousands right now, feeling like my effort is worthwhile and also feeling appreciated, but instead I sit in our youth center by myself, after hours of preparation, hoping that someone will eventually show up.

I do not want to give the impression that local and consistent ministry bears less fruit. It does not. It's just that in offering ongoing service to our local community, family, youth group, rehab center, college, or class, we do not always see the fruit it bears. We sow seeds of love and patience and service, and every now and then, by the grace of God, we get to see a flower grow. Our job, ultimately, is not to reap the fruit but to faithfully sow the seeds, to love when it feels impossible to love, to offer our hearts back to the people when all they seem to do is trample upon it. This too is standing on the edge of a cliff. Sure, there is no limelight, no screaming crowd or media attention, but it is reaching out to souls that would otherwise be lost and therefore, well worth the effort. Ask yourself what you can do to be a presence for God.

1. LIST YOUR RESOURCES. Everything you are and everything you have, including your time, financial resources, talents, and abilities can be used to share the hope you have in Jesus. Make a list of the things you have at your disposal, such as your social media, spare time, gifts, and talents, and speak

to God about how you can use each of these to make Jesus
real in the lives of those around you.

2. STEP OUT IN FAITH. It is not easy to be a witness of Jesus. It
takes courage and requires a death to self. Where can you
step out in faith to help others find joy and salvation? Think
of a situation that happened or is about to happen that could
or would provide you with an opportunity to evangelize.
How would you do it? What if you did do it? What if people
didn't listen? What if people did listen? Maybe after thinking
about it you could even decide to actually step out in faith.

3. CREDIBILITY OF PRESENCE. Where are you at present in your
life? St. Teresa of Calcutta once said that, "charity begins at
home." Are you a witness for Jesus in your family and among
your friends? Do your school or work colleagues see Jesus
in you? It's not about being perfect, but what can you do to
become more of a credible witness of Jesus to them?

Living my vocation means I get to witness to Jesus' unconditional love. While you might not be a priest, as a Christian, your vocation also calls you to be a witness.

EIGHT

God's-Eye View

As we start to come towards the end, it's worth reiterating that I'm far from perfect. I mess up all the time. I embarrass myself often. I post things on social media that come back to bite me. Just the other day, I posted a selfie of myself at the gym. I could not believe how many people accused me of being vain and self-centered. I hope I am not, but maybe I am. Am I? Whatever your answer, I am just so glad that God chooses to love me and allows me to serve him anyway.

Even the great St. Paul messed up, you know. He is considered one of the holiest and most Jesus-like people that ever walked the planet. I have a great devotion to St. Paul. Most Maltese Catholics do, as we owe our Catholic faith to him. He was on his way to Rome on a big ship when it got caught in a storm and he was shipwrecked on Malta (see Acts 28). He performed miracles, healed the sick, and preached about Jesus. This guy was extraordinary, yet he doubted too. He was messed up, just like you and me. In his letter to the Romans, St. Paul says, "I do not understand what I do. For what I want to do, I do not do, but what I hate I do" (Rom 7:15).

Read that verse again. Do you sympathize with him? The words of the great St. Paul could so very much be my own words. I am a priest, and people expect that I should have all the answers and be all-righteous and holy and have everything in order, but I don't. I am often selfish and sometimes I don't think things through. I plan to do good for others but often get too busy with my own plans. I sometimes offend people, yet I often don't know what I did to offend them.

I don't have all the answers either. People assume that priests know everything about God and that they know and can interpret all the teachings of the Church in an instant. Most of us don't and can't. In fact, the more I walk with God, the less I know, and the more I learn, the more questions I have. I doubt. I doubt a lot. Possibly more than many. I don't know everything about God, but the very little I *do* know is enough to keep me chasing after him.

More often than not, when you respond to God's invitation to follow him, he will not immediately make you perfect and sinless, nor will he cause you to suddenly live in a constant state of hope and bliss. Maybe God, because he sure is able, will suddenly heal you from your addiction, cancer, or depression, but maybe, just maybe, he will not. Life with God definitely has its ups, but it has its downs too. In a relationship with Jesus, empowered by his Holy Spirit and sustained by his Body, the Church, life will continue to have its crosses, but you will find strength you never knew you had to pick up your cross and joyfully follow him. With God beside you, you will be able to see and experience the world from a different and higher perspective.

There's something about you
that calms my weary soul

from the song
"Something about You"

When I was growing up, my parents used to take my sister and I to the Sunday *monti*, the street markets, in Valletta. The markets were on a long street and consisted of a series of stalls set up right at the entrance of the capital city. The street merchants would sell books, clothes, and toys, and right next to the toys they would sell fresh fish, live rabbits, and both live and dead poultry. Once you reached the rabbit stall, you could smell the wares of another market vendor cooking and selling *imqaret*, traditional Maltese deep-fried date cakes. There would be thousands of people trying to bargain with the different vendors for the best prices. It was noisy, smelly, busy, and wonderful.

I remember one occasion when I was very young. My brother was not yet born, and Rachel was two years old. My mother carried her in her arms as we wandered through the market. Rachel was wearing a pretty white polka dot dress. I was walking with my father, holding his hand, and dodging the buses and cars and the multitude of people on the busy streets. There was chaos.

My sister decided that she wanted to walk too. My mother put her down, but Rachel didn't want to hold Mum's hand. She wanted to walk alone. My mother left her to walk alone as she desired, but she never took her eyes off her. Eventually, Rachel sensed her freedom and ran ahead, excited about her newly attained independence. Her excitement soon turned to fear as she realized the pure chaos that surrounded her. She could see table legs and the legs of people coming towards her and then walking away from her as the roiling mass of humanity closed in on her. Closer to the ground, the smells were rancid, and fish and animal parts were falling off tables as the stallholders cleaned the animals for sale. There were so many loud noises and distractions. She kept running but soon began to panic in the chaos and confusion around her. She felt vulnerable and alone, not realizing that Mum was right behind her, watching her every step.

As she ran on, she lost confidence and suddenly tripped into a dirty puddle. Her beautiful white dress was now stained and drenched. It quickly turned black and was slimy, smelly, and ugly. She began to cry and lifted her hands towards the sky for Mum to pick her up.

My mother instinctively ran towards her, and with all of her might, she grabbed her and pulled her straight into her chest, close and secure, to reassure her that she was not alone. She didn't worry that Rachel's dress was dirty and that it would dirty her own. She just wanted to make sure that Rachel wasn't hurt, injured, or afraid. Rachel calmed down as Mum wiped away her tears, and she soon stopped crying as she started to feel secure, confident, and safe again.

It didn't take long before she was smiling at the little rabbits in cages and the toys on a nearby table.

What was an absolute disaster suddenly made sense and became exciting. Just moments earlier, she was overcome by a sense of hopelessness and despair, but she now felt secure, safe, and almost invincible because Mum was there to protect her. Life was exciting because she had a new perspective. She could see the world through Mum's eyes.

In fact, that is how she was meant to see the world the whole time.

At the age of two, she was not designed to walk on her own. She didn't even need to be alone, but she insisted on walking by herself, and Mum allowed her to. Although she knew she was not capable, my mother respected Rachel's free will and her desire to try independence, but even then, she never took her eyes off her little child. She was never far behind. All Rachel had to do was ask, and she would have been right back in Mum's arms.

The strength and confidence Rachel had in Mum's arms had nothing to do with her own abilities, strengths, or even her inabilities and weaknesses but everything to do with Mum. Her strength comes from the love and care that Mum had for Rachel.

This is how it is with God. You and I were not created to walk in this world alone. However, God respects our free will, and should we want to journey through life alone, he will allow us, but even then, he is never far behind. Walking alone, we cannot see the world or experience freedom and the joy of this life to the extent that God has created us to. Away from this we cannot live life in the abundance that God has for us (see John 10:10). At the moment we are ready to admit that we need God's help, we can raise our hands in surrender to him, and he will run towards us and lift us into his arms. From there, strong and secure, we will be able to see the world from God's eyes, just the way we were created to see it. Even there we may go through the valley of the shadow of darkness, but walking in a relationship with God and attached to his Body, the Church, we will never need to fear any trial or evil because he will be there with you, holding you close and carrying you to his eye view (see Psalm 23:4).

≈

Allow me, if I may, to talk about another awesome saint: St. Peter. He is also one of the greats. I love St. Peter. He reminds me so much of myself. He always seemed to put his foot in it, and it seems the only time he ever got his foot out was to change feet. He was so bad at times that even Jesus accused him of being an instrument of Satan (see Matthew 16:23).

One time he messed up *big*. He loved Jesus and at one point he was absolutely determined to defend and die for

him (see Matthew 26:35), but when he was given the opportunity to put his money where his mouth was, he failed
miserably and denied Jesus not once, like Judas, not twice,
but *three* times. Like St. Paul, St. Peter hated that he did the
very thing he was determined not to do; so much so that
when he realized how bad he messed up he broke down in
tears (see Matthew 26:75). The extraordinary St. Peter was
so . . . ordinary!

The good news is that the story of St. Peter does not
end here. There is more to this story (see John 21). After
the torture and death of Jesus, St. Peter went back to his
old job. He was tired and disillusioned, and he was angry
and disappointed in himself. He went out fishing, trying to
get his mind off things, when suddenly, out of nowhere,
Jesus appeared. You can imagine the shock, the confusion,
and the awkwardness of such a meeting. The last time they
made eye contact was after they both realized that Peter was
not the friend he said he would be. Now Jesus was standing in front of Peter once again. Peter jumped in the water,
swam to shore, and had a meal with Jesus. After the meal,
the conversation started. There was a big elephant in the
room and Peter wasn't going to be the one to bring it up.

Jesus indulged him. "Hey, Peter."

Peter looked up.

"Do you love me more than these?"

Now this sounds very little like pointing out the elephant in the room at a first glance, but believe me, it was!

The New Testament was written in Greek. The Greeks
were the romantics of the time, just like the Maltese are
today (although the French and the Italians may debate
that). According to C. S. Lewis in his book *The Four Loves*,
the Greeks had four words for love. In English, we have
one: "love." For the sake of my point here, I am going to
mention two of them.

The first is *agape* (ἀγάπη) which is an unconditional love. There is no greater love than this, and the greatest expression of this love is to die for someone (see John 15:13), as Jesus did for you and for me.

Then there is *philia* (φιλία). This is the love of a mate, a brother, or sister. It's a deep friendship. Not nearly as perfect as *agape*, but love nonetheless.

Let us get back to St. Peter and Jesus. Jesus asks Peter. "Simon Peter, son of John, do you *agapas* me more than these?"

Peter would have felt horrible. He had three opportunities to show that he loved Jesus unconditionally, but three times he failed to lay down his life. And this was only three days ago. It was now Peter's turn to respond. "Yes, Lord," he said, "you know that I *philio se*."

Burn!

It would be like a married couple on the morning after their wedding. The wife turns to her new husband and says, "Darling, I love you" and her beloved responds, "Aw, I like you too."

Ouch!

Peter knew his limitations. He was fully aware of his failure to love Jesus as he should. Jesus asked him if he now loved him unconditionally, but Peter, being honest with himself, could not claim that he did. "Jesus, I am not ready to die for you; to love you perfectly, but I do love you as a friend. You want me to love you up here, but this little love, down here, is all I have to offer."

Jesus does not reject the little he had, but tells him that with that small amount he could "take care of my sheep" (Jn 21:16).

This is so encouraging. Like Peter, Jesus does not wait for you to be perfect and without sin to serve him. Jesus asked him the same question, and Peter once again reminded

Jesus that he had *philio* love. Jesus responded, "Take care of my sheep."

The third time Jesus changes his tone. "Simon Peter, son of John, do you *philio* me?" Jesus is clearly accepting the little Peter has to offer. This imperfect love. All Peter had to offer was a mess, and you and I know how the story ends.

According to history, years later St. Peter was martyred for his faith in Jesus. He was crucified, upside down. Jesus told him that he would be.

> "Very truly I tell you, when you were younger you dressed yourself and went where you wanted; but when you are old you will stretch out your hands, and someone else will dress you and lead you where you do not want to go." Jesus said this to indicate the kind of death by which Peter would glorify God. Then he said to him, "Follow me!" (Jn 21:18–19)

What kind of love was this? It was *agape*. Peter spent his life following the risen Christ, and as he walked with him, Jesus perfected the imperfect offering he made that morning by the water.

≋

What do you have to offer? Maybe like me all you have is a *mess*. A bunch of skeletons in your closet and dry bones in your hands. Well, as we discussed right at the start, offer that to God and watch him turn your *mess* into a beautiful *message*. Let him into your life, and follow him. Serve him too. Don't wait to be holy and to have things in order before you do. Say yes, and let him set your life in order and make you holy.

I am a work in progress. One day, as I follow Jesus, I hope to be holier and perfect, but for now God knows that all I have to offer is this mess. "Jesus, if you can take this mess and make something out of it, here I am."

I pray this every day at Mass, as I break the Eucharist in preparation for the distribution of Communion. I serve God and I love doing so, but it has never been and never will be about how good and holy I am but always about who God is—a merciful and patient God who says to me, "Feed my sheep."

Whether you are called to the priesthood or religious life or not, and whether you are young or old, gay or straight, healthy or sick, able or disabled, Jesus invites you to do the same: to be his witness in a world that is in desperate need of his unconditional love. This is your baptismal mandate. As you received his Holy Spirit on your Baptism day, you were empowered and commissioned to know, love, and serve Jesus.

> But you will receive power when the Holy Spirit comes on you; and you will be my witnesses in Jerusalem, and in all Judea and Samaria, and to the ends of the earth. (Acts 1:8)

To evangelize cannot and should not be the work of the elite few. Especially today. You have as much a call and need to evangelize as I do and the pope does. You need to get over your sense of unworthiness. You will never be worthy enough. No one ever is. The reality is that many will listen to you before they listen to me, a nun, or the pope.

There was a famous philosopher by the name of Søren Kierkegaard. He tells a story of a circus that visited a town. The villagers were enjoying the circus show when a fire broke out backstage. The circus performers tried desperately to put out the fire but they could not. The ringleader asked if someone could go out to tell the crowd about the fire so that they could evacuate the tent. The clown volunteered.

In his clown costume, makeup, and big red nose he got onto his tiny bicycle to get to the ring as fast as he could. He cycled out to the center of the tent shouting and pressing his comedically oversized horn to warn the people.

"Fire, fire!" he shouted, as he pedalled round and round the stage.

The people laughed and applauded. "Do it again!" they shouted.

"Fire, fire! Evacuate the tent or you're all going to die!"

The applause was even greater. The audience believed it was a joke, a skit by the clown. The story ends tragically, with every member of the audience perishing inside that tent.

This is how it is in the Kingdom of God. This world needs to hear the Gospel, but it often comes from people all dressed up and in official and qualified positions in the Church. People applaud and others ask for more. Some stop listening, bored, as they have seen the same show over and over again. Your friends, family, colleagues, and acquaintances need to know the way to Jesus, the author of their salvation, but maybe the ones in costume are not the one to give the message: maybe *you* are the one God is calling to be a witness in your school or workplace. You do this best by the way you love and serve them, even if you have no reason to do so.

A friend of mine was in a supermarket one day. It was a Friday evening and the place was busy. As he did his grocery shopping, he noticed a woman with three little children. One was sitting in the trolley, another was in her arms, and the other was throwing a tantrum. As he cried, he was punching the mum's leg. She was doing her best, trying to juggle the children and not to forget all the things she had to buy.

As they checked out, the woman was two people ahead of my mate in the line and in between them was a man in his forties. The woman put her items through, visibly exhausted, still trying to herd her three children as the check-out lady scanned her goods. "That will be $150 please. Will you be paying by cash or card?"

The young mother began searching for her purse. "Cash please," she said, as she continued to search, this time more frantically. A look of horror crossed her face when she realized she must have forgotten her purse. "I am so sorry, but I left my money at home." Her voice was barely a whisper as she fought back tears.

There was a long line waiting behind her and she was so embarrassed. Almost immediately, the man behind her said, "I will pay this for you."

"No," she replied, "you don't need to do that."

"I want to," he said, insistently.

She reluctantly accepted and asked for his details to pay him back.

"I do not want any payment. I want to do this for you," he told her gently.

She looked confused and got quite emotional at that point. "Why?" she asked. "Why are you doing this?"

His reply moved my Catholic friend.

"Because I am a Christian and I am grateful for what Jesus has done for me, and now I want to help you."

She gave him a hug and then made her way to the parking lot.

This was an incredible witness. I wish I could do that—just stand at the checkout counter and pay for people's groceries and say, "I did this because I love Jesus"—but I can't financially afford to do that. I'm not sure that many can.

What I can do is clear up random trollies from the parking lot, help someone change a tire, put the weights back at the gym (even if I didn't get them out in the first place), and tidy up after myself so that others don't have to. I may not have the opportunity to say that I am doing it for Jesus, but I can be a gentle example of love and excellence and, in my heart, learn to do all things for Jesus.

You can also evangelize through a life of excellence and humility. You can speak about your love of God when the occasion arises, but a lot of our opportunities to evangelize are small and will often go unnoticed. Whatever you choose to do, do it *not* to be noticed and appreciated but to serve people, the community, and his Body, the Church.

There is a famous quote that is often attributed to St. Francis of Assisi: "Preach the Gospel at all times. Use words if necessary." This is true, but very often we *do* have to use words. We need to tell people about Jesus and his love for them. We cannot be quiet for fear of offending someone. Jesus used words, the apostles used words, St. Francis used words, and so should you, and so will I. I'm not talking about preaching on a street corner, but telling people what Jesus has done for you, should you get the opportunity.

If they know you are a Catholic, people will ask questions. I often hear questions like, "If God is a good and loving God, then why does he allow suffering?" or "Who created God?" or "Why do you believe in God?"

This is why you need to spend time reflecting and studying your faith. There is a lot of help out there if you wanted to know some answers. Some require personal reflection, and others require research and understanding. Make time to study your faith for the times you need to share it or even defend it: "Always be prepared to give an answer to everyone who asks you to give the reason for the hope that you have" (1 Pt 3:15).

I believe that we need to know our faith, and that is why I produce weekly YouTube videos with answers to tough questions, but I also acknowledge that sometimes we just cannot know the right answer. I don't have the answers when a young girl asks me why she's so depressed or when a young married man asks why God allowed him to get leukemia.

While I don't have all the answers, the good news is that I know someone who does: Jesus. I sit with people who have these tough questions, lost for words, and I pray with them, cry with them, and point them to Jesus. I cannot heal them, save them, or console their spirit, but God can — a God whom I trust in spite of the many unanswered questions that myself and those around me have.

Reach out to the poor, speak out for the voiceless, and pray. All this is impossible without prayer. It will take courage, and you will be given the grace once you step out in faith, but don't wait until you are worthy, theologically educated, or have your life all together before you take up this call. If I waited for any of this, I would never have stepped out, nor would I step out today.

> But God chose the foolish things of the world to shame the wise; God chose the weak things of the world to shame the strong. God chose the lowly things of this world and the despised things — and the things that are not — to nullify the things that are, so that no one may boast before him. (1 Cor 1:27–29)

I've read that God doesn't call the qualified, he qualifies the called! Think about some of the great God-servants in the Bible, as this anonymous quotation does:

> Jacob was a cheater, Peter had a temper, David had an affair, Noah got drunk, Jonah ran from God, Paul was a murderer, Gideon was insecure, Miriam was a gossip, Martha was a worrier, Thomas was a doubter, Sara was

impatient, Elijah was moody, Moses stuttered, Abraham
was old . . . and Lazarus was dead.

God invites us to come as we are, messed up, broken, and
insecure. God invites us to feed his sheep and to follow him.
It is as we partner with God in his Kingdom and follow him
that we become as he calls us to "Be perfect, therefore, as
your heavenly Father is perfect" (Mt 5:48).

Being called as we are, imperfect and in need of a Savior
ourselves, we become more of a surrendered instrument in
the master's hands. God is the potter, and we are the clay.
"Does the clay say to the potter, 'What are you making?'
Does your work say, 'The potter has no hands'?" (Is 45:9).

The world needs God, and we need God. In fact, God is
all we need. You see, even though we need to let the world
know of the love of Jesus, our primary vocation is not to
evangelize. Our primary call is to become holy ourselves—
to become like Jesus. To become like Jesus is to surrender
to his will. It takes a lifetime to surrender to God, and even
then, we still need God's mercy.

Fr. Chris, my old mentor and friend who pulled me
through tough times, taught me a lot about surrender. He
loved and served God beautifully, but he was by no means
perfect. He himself would have been quick to admit to his
imperfections. One of them was that he was very, very
proud of his intellect. He was a very clever man, and he
made sure that people knew it. In the middle of a relaxing
conversation among priests, for example, he would bring
up a controversial subject to get an argument going. He
loved a heated argument. He would argue just to prove a
point. The whole room would be steaming, but he would
leave the room feeling proud and confident that he won the
argument. I eventually learned the art of avoiding certain

conversations and arguments with him. Maybe that is why we got on so well.

As he was dying from cancer, he moved into my house so that the St. Kilian's priests, staff, and I could care for him. As his health deteriorated, I saw him grow in holiness. In his last days, and probably because of the cancer and the pain medication, he began to lose all sense of logic. He would mumble words and experience few moments of clarity. The night he died, I prayed for him as I did every night he was in my care. After I finished the prayer, he said his own prayer which made perfect sense. The last words he prayed were, "Jesus give me the grace and the humility to accept the loss of my intellect." Those are the last words he ever spoke.

He died that night.

At the end of the day, all we need is Jesus, not our gifts, strengths, or even our health. These are all wonderful, God-given things, but their purpose in our lives is to order us towards him. This, when all has been said and done, is the greatest witness we can give: for the world to see us surrendered to God. Look around you and reflect on what you see.

1. EXTRAORDINARY ORDINARY. Through your Baptism, God has placed an extraordinary call over your life. The way we respond to that call can be pretty ordinary. Spend some time thanking God for this call over your life and ask for the grace not to seek success but to serve this call with extraordinary faithfulness.

2. WITNESS. You are called to be a witness. Think of ways you can carry out that call in your day-to-day life. How can you serve others, even in small things? Think of ways you can serve him that may go unnoticed, such as picking up a neighbor's tipped-over garbage bin or paying someone's expired parking meter. Think of a way you can talk about and point someone to Jesus.

3. GOD'S-EYE VIEW. So many times we seek to walk alone, without God and his Body, the Church. Spend some time thinking about times and ways you have pridefully walked away from God and ask for forgiveness, knowing that he walks right behind you waiting to lift you up back into his arms as you surrender to him.

My journey isn't done, and I still need to seek God's will for my music, my ministry, and my life.

NINE

By the Grace of God

I wrote the song "Only by Grace" after watching a documentary on the National Geographic channel. It was a program about eagles, but I don't remember the details of the episode, just the part where the mother eagle was teaching her babies how to fly.

Just picture it.

Mum and her baby eagles are in their nest on a cliff with a five-star view to rival any hotel. It's a beautiful sunny day with a light breeze, and Dad's out gathering some fish to feed the family. The little eagles don't appreciate how good they have it. Life for them is nothing but bliss with two protective parents looking after their every need.

Dad returns to the nest with a little fish, the birds open their mouths, and they are fed. After feeding the family, Dad returns to the ocean to do some more hunting. After Mum settles the children she stands at the edge of the cliff and seemingly takes in the view, but she is thinking, planning.

She suddenly turns around, opens her wings and violently throws the eaglets out of the nest. The three little birds are falling to their death, but just before they hit the ground Mum swoops down, picks them up, and puts them back into the nest.

They look stunned, confused, and flustered all at once. Their little hearts are beating so fast and hard that you can see the feathers on their chest moving.

"What just happened? Why did Mum just do that? We could have died!" they say to each other.

Before they have a chance to even look at Mum, she opens her wings again and they are once more falling to their deaths.

Just minutes before life was perfect. They had done nothing wrong. They did not deserve this cruelty, this abandonment and rejection. Their short lives are now flashing before their eyes.

Then, it happens.

As he is falling, one of the eaglets fixes his eyes on his mother soaring high above and it suddenly clicks. He opens his little wings and stops falling. He opens them wider and begins to soar.

"Look at me!" he squeaks his siblings. "Look at me! I can fly! Open your wings!"

Only by grace the eagle's fly
By that same grace
You'll lift me high

from the song
"Only by Grace"

One copied him, and then the other, ceasing their plummeting doom. They are now soaring, rising up on the current, taking in the views, basking in unbelievable freedom. They cannot believe it. The most tragic of situations—a time when they felt abandoned and alone, the worst hour of their lives—turned out to be the moment they became all they were created to be: soaring eagles, just like Mum.

God meets us in our darkness and tears down the walls of fear and brokenness and lifts us to become all that we were created to be: just like his Son, Jesus. This is grace.

This is exactly what he did for me.

When I had reached the end of myself, which we all do at some point, I was lifted towards a God who drew me into a personal relationship. Grace allowed me to open my God-given wings, and now I soar. My flight is not something I have earned, nor is it something I deserve. It is only by grace that this eagle flies as I attempt to lift up my eyes to God and keep them fixed on him.

≈

God did it for me, and he wants to do it for you. How? First of all, you need to understand who you are, just like the eaglet needed to understand who he was. He was the child of a majestic eagle and capable of becoming just like her. You are a child of God and capable of becoming like Jesus. You were created for greatness, formed with a purpose to be a world-changer, to be a history-maker, to be a champion, to be a saint. Get to know Jesus through prayer and in his Word, and fix your eyes on him. Seek him in his Body, the Church, and once you find him, hold on. Hold on to Jesus with every fiber of your being and show the world what you have found.

Secondly, choose love, not fear. 1 John 4:18 says, "there is no fear in love," and that "perfect love drives out all fear." Stop making excuses. Stop giving into fear. God will not condemn you. He will not reject you. He will never abandon you. Trust God and jump out of the nest of fear, believing that he will catch you. God has a great purpose for your life but you have a choice: to stay in the nest of comfort, fear, and shame or get up and face your fear and become all that God has created you to be. God will be right there beside you, to protect and inspire you (see Psalm 91:8–15).

But what if God won't catch me? But what if I fail? But I don't have the time or energy for it right now! But what will my family and friends think? But I am too scared.

Jesus invites you to live in true joy, freedom, and hope. He calls you to inspire others to do the same. Don't let your big "but" get in the way. I dread to think of the countless people called to soar above the clouds that are still sitting on their big "buts" in their cozy nests. Get up, let God break those chains of fear that hold you down, and get rid of those big "buts"!

The best way to get rid of a big butt is by doing squats. Why on earth am I now talking about squats? I want to try and explain how you can get rid of your big "buts" using the same process of getting rid of big butts. Squats. Have you ever done a squat? Doing proper squats are tough and painful, but if you persist you will see results pretty fast. There are three necessary parts to a good squat exercise:

1. Find your center of gravity.
2. Get your butt to the ground.
3. Get up again.

How do you find your center of gravity? If you do not have a good center of gravity when doing a squat, you will lose your balance and possibly injure yourself. You need to have a strong foothold, something that will not move or shake, something that will stand strong even when every-thing around you is unstable. What is your life's center of gravity? What do you have to stand on when the world around you shakes?

My center of gravity is my relationship with Jesus and his Church. Seek to know, love, and serve him with all of your heart. When I had to move away from my family to Australia, when Bishop Joe and Fr. Chris died, and when I find life too much to handle, I still find strength and joy as I hold on to Jesus. My family cannot be my center of gravity, nor can my friends. My music certainly is a comfort, but when all is said and done, it cannot save me. In my relationship with Jesus and his Church, I have a strength that can help me survive every storm.

Have you ever gone into a shop to choose a rose for your valentine or for your mother on Mother's Day? I have. Around Mother's Day there are thousands of red roses in flower shops across Australia. What most people consider when choosing the rose is the brightness of the petals and how open the petals are. They will check the scent and make sure that there are no bugs. Very few would walk in and choose the rose because of the stem, no matter how impressive it is.

Think of it this way. The petals represent our relationship with God, and the stem represents the tradition and ritual of the church. For many, all they know is the stem. It is strong and sturdy. It has thorns. Some are happy with that and feel safe with that. I did not. Maybe you don't either. As a child, I knew about the stem, but nobody ever told me about the petals. And you know what? The stem was fine at first, but when I became a teenager the thorns started to cause me discomfort. Eventually it was like I was being whipped with the stem.

Do your religion homework. Go to Mass. Don't have sex. Share your food.

By the time I was fourteen, I didn't want to have anything to do with the stem. It was painful, judgmental, and inconvenient. I walked away.

At the age of sixteen, I got introduced to the petals. I could not believe how beautiful they were. The scent was unbelievable. All this time I had only ever seen the stem but never the petals. I wanted more. I began to fall in love, but all I wanted was the petals. I didn't want the stem. I would go to youth group but not to Mass, and I didn't pray. I did not carry out any works of charity, nor was I interested in learning about the traditions and teachings of the Church.

Eventually, the petals began to dry out and fall apart.

That was until I began to pray and discovered the riches and beauty and necessity of the stem. The stem was necessary to hold the petals together, to protect it and give it life. The thorns protected the rose from predators and allowed the petals to thrive.

The petals and the stem are incomplete without each other. Both are necessary. The stem without the rose petals seems lifeless and torturous to many. The petals alone are attractive but can't survive for long without being fed nutrients by the stem.

We need a relationship with God, but we need the believing community, the sacraments, God's Word, and the teachings and tradition of the Church in order to grow, survive, and thrive as one Body in Christ.

Going back to the squat exercises, point number two was to get your butt to the ground. Once you have a solid center of gravity, the next thing to do is focus and get your butt to the ground. Don't be afraid to get all the way down to the floor. At that point, you may feel like you're going to lose your balance and fall, but this is where you need to trust your center of gravity. Down there you may feel defeated, but do not underestimate the power that is within you. "I can do all this through him who gives me strength" (Phil 4:13).

No matter how good our intentions are and no matter how hard we try, we will all occasionally get our butts to the ground. We will all feel like we have failed and go through times of doubt. In moments such as these, we need to trust that God, in his mercy, will never abandon us and will give us the strength to get back up again. There is no mess too big, no sin too great, and no distance too far for the arms of God to reach you. No matter who you are, where you're from, or what you have done, there is always room for you at the foot of the Cross of Jesus. It's a place of infinite love and mercy. You need to understand and believe this if you are to muster the strength to get back up again.

In moments when our butts are to the floor and the weight of life is pressing against you, thoughts of doubt and giving up are inevitable. Doubt is part of growing in faith. It is not wrong, nor is it a sin to doubt, but you need to fight that doubt and not let it control you. God said that he will be with you always (see Matthew 28:20), and he will. God said it, you act on it, and that settles it! Both sinners and saints fall to the ground. Sinners stay there and saints muster up the courage to get back up again.

And the last part of the squat exercise *is* to get up again. This is the hardest part of the squat. This is the part where your body, mind, and soul need to be focused entirely on getting that weight up off the ground. At this point, you have to face your fear and do it scared.

The world around you might think you're crazy, and perhaps they don't understand why you're doing what you're doing. You don't have all the answers. Doubt may still be in your mind, but you keep going. Keep pushing against gravity, and know that God will give you the strength to get up again.

Getting up again is about understanding the purpose and plan God has for your life. As you raise yourself, you may not have all the answers, so in humility surrender to God and lift others with you as you point to the one who holds you in his arms: Jesus.

≋

If God can do it for me, he can do it for you. God broke through my hard and broken heart, took that heart to his, and by his grace, has used it to impact the lives of others. I could never have pictured it happening, but it did. It happened in ways that I could not have dreamed of, and the thing is I know that I have not even scratched the surface of what God has in store for the rest of my life. It took an act of surrender. Having reached the end of myself, I cried out to a loving God who lifted me upon his shoulders. All is fresh and all is new every day as I continue to try to surrender to his will. Sometimes I succeed and many times I fail, and it often feels like one step forward and two steps back, but at each small step forward God runs towards me and carries me the distance of a race which I hope to run to the end. I know that I do not run this race alone. I run with countless people who are striving, like me, to know, love, and be faithful witnesses to a personal, loving God.

> Therefore, since we are surrounded by such a great cloud of witnesses, let us throw off everything that hinders and the sin that so easily entangles. And let us run with perseverance the race marked out for us, fixing our eyes on Jesus, the pioneer and perfector of faith. (Heb 12:1–2)

In the Bible, God has many names, each name defining an attribute of God. *El Shaddai* (Lord God Almighty), *Jehovah-Raah* (the Lord My Shepherd), *Adonai* (Lord, Master), *El Olam* (the Everlasting God), but one of my all-time favorites is *Baal Perazim*. This is translated to "Lord of the Breakthrough" (see 2 Samuel 5:20). I love that title and regularly address God by that name because it encourages me to look back in gratitude at what God has done for me. It also serves as a reminder that he is perfectly able to work that same grace in the lives of others.

That's right, Baal Perazim is able to break through any wall in *your* life: the wall of sin, depression, anxiety, sickness, or heartbreak. He can tear down the walls of anger and addiction, rebellion, loneliness, and fear.

You've seen where I came from. I was a messed-up teenager, trapped in my bedroom with no hope for the future. I like to hope now that I am living my life in the arms of God. I have hope and I have a future. Being held by a loving God, my heart is on fire, and I want only to help you see that you can have this joy and peace too. It goes beyond the feeling of happiness, and it's not dependent on how good and holy you are. Joy and peace come when you realize that you are unconditionally loved by a good and holy God. Even when bad things happen and you fall short of your call to "be perfect, therefore, as your heavenly Father is perfect" (Mt 5:48), God will be with you and will continue to love, hold, and carry you.

Once you truly experience and understand this, then by the grace of God, your life will never be the same again, and your heart will burn to share the Good News with others.

Acknowledgments

This book has been three years in the making. I would like to acknowledge those who have made this dream possible.

God, of course! This book is a documentation of God's love and work in my life.

I thank my parents, Anne and Paul, and my brother, Joseph, and sister, Rachel.

I am filled with gratitude for Dr. John Bonnici Mallia, Padre Giovanni Saccà, and the late Bishop Joe Grech and Fr. Chris Reay for being my life mentors and role models.

I would also like to express my gratitude to Garratt Publishing in Australia and Ave Maria Press in the USA for believing that I had something of substance to offer. Thanks also to Rebecca Wylie at Sage Written Word and to Michelle Rafter for helping me put my thoughts to paper. I would also like to thank Fr. Liam Lawton for patiently and generously working with me in the early stages of this book.

Thanks to Bishop Les Tomlinson and Fr. Rom Hayes for allowing me the time to work on this book. Thank you to my parish community at St. Kilian's and our Stronger Youth for inspiring me to love and serve Jesus.

Fr. Rob Galea is a Catholic speaker, recording artist, songwriter, and priest of the Sandhurst Diocese in Victoria, Australia. Originally from Malta, he travels the world speaking to youth and young adults at schools, parishes, concerts, and conferences such as the Los Angeles Religious Education Congress and the National Catholic Youth Conference. He ministers to more than 200,000 young people annually and has an international presence through weekly posts to his popular YouTube channel.

In 2008, Galea cofounded the Stronger Youth Program, one of Victoria's largest Catholic youth movements. He appeared as a contestant on Australia's version of *The X Factor* in 2015 and sang the English versions of the official 2008 and 2016 World Youth Day songs. Galea has recorded with renowned artists such as pop idol Guy Sebastian, Paulini, Gary Pinto, Natasha Pinto, Ira Losco, and Amelia Farrugia. He has shared the stage with the likes of Matt Maher, Hillsong United, and Darlene Zschech.

http://www.frrobgalea.com
Instagram, YouTube, Vimeo: @frrobgalea
Twitter: @FrRobGalea
Facebook: Fr. Rob Galea

Rev. Liam Lawton is an Irish priest, singer/songwriter, and recording artist.

AVE

AVE MARIA PRESS

Founded in 1865, Ave Maria Press,
a ministry of the Congregation of
Holy Cross, is a Catholic publishing
company that serves the spiritual and
formative needs of the Church and its
schools, institutions, and ministers;
Christian individuals and families; and
others seeking spiritual nourishment.

For a complete listing of titles from

Ave Maria Press

Sorin Books

Forest of Peace

Christian Classics

visit www.avemariapress.com

AVE | AVE MARIA PRESS
Notre Dame, IN
A Ministry of the United States Province of Holy Cross